CENTRALITY AND COMMONALITY

ξ

CENTRALITY AND COMMONALITY: AN ESSAY ON CHUNG-YUNG
三

Tu Wei-ming
二

MONOGRAPH NO. 3 OF THE

SOCIETY FOR ASIAN AND COMPARATIVE PHILOSOPHY

THE UNIVERSITY PRESS OF HAWAII

1976

"Spiritual Dimensions: The Doctrine of the
Mean," in A Source Book in Chinese Philosophy,
transl. and compiled by Wing-tsit Chan (copy-
right (c) 1963 by Princeton University Press;
Princeton Paperback, 1969), pp. 95 through
114. Reprinted by permission of Princeton
University Press.

Tu, Wei-ming.
   Centrality and commonality.

   (Monograph of the Society for Asian and
Comparative Philosophy ; no. 3)
   Includes bibliographical references and
index.
   1. Chung yung. I. Title. II. Series:
Society for Asian and Comparative Philosophy.
Monograph of the Society for Asian and Compara-
tive Philosophy ; no. 3.
PL2473.Z7T8   299'.51282   76-17054
ISBN 0-8248-0447-3

To an original thinker and an inspiring teacher,

Mou Tsung-san

CONTENTS

Chung-yung, commonly known as the Doctrine of the Mean, is a central document in the Confucian tradition. For more than two thousand years, as an important chapter in one of the Five Classics,[1] Chung-yung has continuously been a source of inspiration for the creative mind in Chinese intellectual history.[2] From the time the great Confucian synthesizer Chu Hsi (1130-1200) selected Chung-yung as one of the Four Books,[3] it has exerted an impact on traditional Chinese education as profound as that of the Analects. In premodern times, every Chinese literatus learned the work by heart before he reached adolescence, and from 1313 to 1905 it was a basic text for civil-service examinations. Indeed, the mode of thinking presented in Chung-yung is still readily perceivable as a defining characteristic of many a philosophical reflection in contemporary China.[4]

Although the significance of Chung-yung is widely acknowledged, however, few systematic attempts have been made to analyze the text as a whole. Traditional Chinese and Japanese scholars have assumed that since the integrity of the text as an authentic Confucian classic is beyond question,

the scholar's task is simply to write exegeses on
it. Recent students of Chinese thought, under the
influence of the iconoclastic attacks on Confucianism prevalent since the "new cultural movement" of
May Fourth in 1919, have raised some fundamental
doubts about the cohesiveness of the text. As a
result, quite a few sinologists now believe that
the work is no more than a collection of aphorisms.

My approach to Chung-yung is interpretive
rather than exegetical. This is based on the assumption that the inner logic of Chung-yung cannot be
made explicit merely by a series of commentaries on
its words, sentences, paragraphs, or chapters. Hermeneutical analyses are suggestive and sometimes
enlightening because they help us to gain insight
into the underlying themes of the text, which, in
turn, enable us to understand how the rules of this
particular "language game," to use a current expression, are formulated. To be sure, as a method
of learning we cannot afford to ignore the available
exegetical commentaries on the text, especially
those that are considered standard scholarship on
the subject. But we must progress from commentaries to interpretations so that the meaning of
the text as a whole is also taken into serious consideration.

I should note that the approach in this inquiry
is not intended to be a form of structuralism.

Certainly my purpose is, in part, to make it clear
that there is a deep, integral structure in Chung-
yung and that only through a holistic reading of
the text can one penetrate its surface semantics
and arrive at an appreciation of its inner meanings.
The emphasis on wholeness may give the impression
that the historicity of the text is relegated to
the background. While the primary concern of my
work is to study Chung-yung as the unfolding of a
humanistic vision, I have taken into account issues
concerning the genesis of the text such as authorship and dating. I maintain, however, that although genetic problems are closely related to our
quest for a broad understanding of the text, they
are not to be confused with the problems of the
semantic nucleus around which the symbolic articulations of the text evolve. Indeed, notwithstanding
the danger of intentional fallacy, I would very
much like to associate myself with the hermeneutical
art, which takes as its point of departure that a
central text in a spiritual tradition, far from
being an anthology of isolated statements, is likely
to have an organismic unity of its own.

My task, then, has not been to advocate a fun-
damentalist position on Chung-yung but to explicate
the text through interpretation; since interpretation in this particular connection is not the imposition of a fixed notion of rationality on the

text, but a process of opening oneself up to the text, I felt, even while writing, an acute sense of discovery and a strong need for confirmation. Thus the final product is simply an exploratory essay waiting to be validated or invalidated by the community of scholars in which the pursuit of this type of learning was made meaningful in the first place. My interpretation of Chung-yung consequently is no more than a reenactment of an age-long Confucian ritual. If the reenactment has any objective value at all, it must be intersubjectively confirmed although it can probably never be empirically or positivistically verified.[5]

In this exploratory essay, therefore, I intend to take the traditional assumption seriously and will try to show how the seemingly unconnected aphoristic statements in Chung-yung make sense as integral parts of a coherent thesis on personality, society, and religion. My inquiry begins with a critical examination of the current impression that the contents of the text are varied and that it seems to lack a logically consistent form. I hope to show that the so-called "mystical" aspects of Chung-yung are basically in accord with the Mencian tradition of Confucian thought[6] and that, without in any way rearranging the text, it can be understood and appreciated as the unfolding of an ethicoreligious vision on the inseparability of the Human Way and the Way of Heaven.

Through a symbolic analysis of the three core ideas in the text--chün-tzu (superior man, or profound person), cheng (politics), and ch'eng (sincerity)--I hope to demonstrate that such familiar dichotomies as the tension between self and society and the conflict between ethics and religion are alien to Chung-yung's spiritual orientation. This interpretation will probably unsettle the conventional belief that Confucianism is preeminently a social philosophy or an ethical system. But my purpose is not so much to underscore a few selected elements in Chung-yung as to introduce a new way of analyzing all of its salient features. If my interpretative position is tenable, Chung-yung's reflections on the "profound person" who is engaged in a continual process toward an ever-deepening subjectivity,[7] on society as a "fiduciary community,"[8] rather than as an adversary system, and on "sincerity" as a primary concept in the construction of a "moral metaphysics"[9] will suggest an exceedingly interesting approach to some of the perennial human concerns.

In writing this essay, I have benefited greatly from long discussions with several friends and colleagues. I would like particularly to thank John Ewell, Stephen Hay, Lao Ssu-kuang, Leonard Nathan, Irwin Scheiner, and Frederic Wakeman, Jr.

for their searching criticisms of an earlier version of the study. I owe a debt of gratitude to Paige Wickland for her editorial help. I am also grateful to Floris Sakamoto for her kind assistance in preparing the manuscript for publication. My deepest appreciation goes to Professor Wing-tsit Chan whose pioneering work on Chinese philosophy has been an important source of inspiration for my work, and it is in this connection that I wish to acknowledge my indebtedness to the Princeton University Press for permission to use Professor Chan's annotated translation of <u>Chung-yung</u> in his <u>Source Book in Chinese Philosophy</u> (1973).

Tu Wei-ming

CENTRALITY AND COMMONALITY

CHAPTER 1

The Text

Perhaps the most difficult problem confronting
the reader of Chung-yung is its mode of expression.
Instead of using analytical models in an argumentative dialogue, Chung-yung's language, like that of
the Confucian Analects, is aphoristic. And it is
tempting to formulate one's initial interpretive response by focusing on the apparent simplicity of its
overall design. But the statements in Chung-yung are
integral parts of a complicated structure, involving
many levels of intellectual sophistication. Of
course, a statement in Chung-yung can be easily ab-
stracted from its context and still make good sense
as a quotable maxim. In fact, the work has for years
been treated, by Chinese scholars as well as sinologists in the West, as a collection of proverbs. But
as a philosophical work in the opinion of Wing-tsit
Chan, it is "perhaps the most philosophical in the
whole body of ancient Confucian literature"[1] it has
an integrity of its own. Indeed, the "literal" reading of isolated passages will not get us very far,
for unless the aphoristic formulations are understood
in their interrelatedness, the dangers of misinterpretation are acute. It may be helpful to begin our

2

discussion of <u>Chung-yung</u> with a close analysis of
the way its structure works, using as our example
the first chapter of the text. It reads, in its
entirety, as follows:

> What Heaven imparts to man is called human
> nature. To follow human nature is called
> the Way. Cultivating the Way is called
> teaching. The Way cannot be separated from
> us for a moment. What can be separated from
> us is not the Way. Therefore the profound
> person is cautious over what he does not see
> and apprehensive over what he does not hear.
> There is nothing more visible than what is
> hidden and nothing more manifest than what is
> subtle. Therefore the profound person is
> watchful over himself when he is alone. Be-
> fore the feelings of pleasure, anger, sorrow,
> and joy are aroused it is called centrality.
> When the feelings are aroused and each and
> all attain due measure and degree, it is
> called harmony. Centrality is the great
> foundation of the world, and harmony is its
> universal path. To cultivate[2] centrality
> and harmony with thoroughness is the way to
> bring heaven and earth to their proper place
> and all things their proper nourishment.
> [I:1-5][3]

<u>Chung-yung</u> begins with three definitional
statements: "What Heaven imparts to man is called
human nature. To follow human nature is the Way.
Cultivating the Way is called teaching." Obviously, the statements are presented not as freshly argued propositions but as notions which, from <u>Chung-</u>

yung's point of view, are self-evidently true. We will probe into the philosophical implications of these assertions later; we note here that it is Chung-yung's position that heaven-endowed human nature defines what the Way is, which in turn characterizes what teaching ought to be. Having defined the Way as the unfolding of human nature and having characterized teaching as the manifestation of the Way, Chung-yung continues: "The Way cannot be separated from us for a moment. What can be separated from us is not the Way." In terms of the mode of expression, these two lines seem to have significantly departed from the first three statements; they are not definitional but sententious utterances, stressing the inseparability of the Way and our ordinary existence.

Then, without any warning that the form of articulation is being shifted to yet another plane, Chung-yung further asserts: "Therefore the profound person is cautious over what he does not see and apprehensive over what he does not hear." On the surface, the caution and apprehension of the profound person do not seem to be connected with the inseparability of the Way and our ordinary existence. One wonders how the word "therefore" functions in this context. The two lines immediately following add to the puzzling semantic situation: "There is nothing more visible than what is hidden and nothing more manifest than what is subtle. Therefore the profound person is watchful over himself when he is alone." However, if these statements are examined, not as a linear argumentative procedure but as a pattern of thought, we can detect their point of orientation as a whole. Indeed, they all seem to focus on what may be called the subjectivity of the profound person.

The caution and apprehension of the profound person are connected with the inseparability of the Way and our ordinary existence because if the Way is inherent in our human nature, the actualization of it depends upon our self-knowledge. The profound person whose self-knowledge is deeper than most of us is, therefore, particularly concerned with the interiority of the self; what he neither sees nor hears is precisely the inner self upon which the manifestation of the Way is based. We can perhaps describe the transition as follows: Since the way that can be departed from our ordinary human existence, such as the spiritual way in Moism and the natural way in Taoism, is not the Confucian Way in Chung-yung; the profound person, as the paradigmatic example of Confucian personality, must be acutely aware of the inner processes through which his humanity is to be manifested as the Way. Therefore, it is quite conceivable that the profound person's caution and apprehension over his inner self is the natural consequence of his awareness that the Way is inseparable from his human nature.

Accordingly, the next line, "There is nothing more visible than what is hidden and nothing more manifest than what is subtle," can be taken as a different way of expressing the same idea: although the inner self is hidden and subtle as an object of perception in the audiovisual sense, it is most "visible" and "manifest" to the conscientious and reflective mind of the profound person. It is in this connection that Chung-yung declares that "the profound person is watchful over himself when he is alone."

The emphasis on personal knowledge as an experiental confirmation of the inner self becomes the main concern of the second part of the first chapter in Chung-yung: "Before the feelings of pleasure, anger, sorrow, and joy are aroused it is called centrality. When the feelings are aroused and each and all attain due measure and degree, it is called harmony. Centrality is the great foundation of the world, and harmony is its universal path." The relationship between "centrality and harmony" (chung-ho) has for centuries been one of the key issues in Confucian philosophy;[4] we will examine it at some length later in our discussion. Suffice it to note here that in Chung-yung's mode of thought the self-cultivation of the profound person is by no means a private affair, because an experience of the orig-

inal tranquility of human nature is an experience
not only of quiescence before the basic feelings
are aroused in the psychological sense but also of
the ultimate reality, or in Chung-yung's words, the
great foundation of the world, in the ontological
sense. Similarly, the harmonization of one's basic
feelings in accordance with the standards of the
human community is a manifestation of the path of
being human in the ethicoreligious sense as well as
in the psychosocial. Indeed, it is vitally important to note that the unity of man and heaven is a
fundamental theme that underlies all of Chung-yung's
philosophical articulations. Understandably, the
first chapter concludes with the statement: "To
cultivate centrality and harmony with thoroughness
is the way to bring heaven and earth to their proper
place and all things their proper nourishment."

Even in this preliminary inquiry into the first
chapter, we can see that Chung-yung's mode of expression is significantly different from what we normally
consider to be rhetorical art. The technique of persuasion seems completely lacking. Statements are not
presented as components in an elaborate argument
structure. On the contrary, the logical connections
among them are not explicit, and the semantic move-
ments from the earlier to the later terms are not
constructed in a linear progression. However, if
the first chapter of Chung-yung fails remarkably in

rhetoric, its method of presentation, with multiple
layers of meaning in a highly compact linguistic
formulation, is reminiscent of the spirit of poet-
ics. Actually, as a point of orientation, we can
at least suggest that the poetic mode, with emphasis
on internal human resonance, is much more pertinent
to Chung-yung than the rhetoric intention of influ-
encing the reader by the art of persuasion. An important thing to bear in mind, then, is the unity
of experience to be acquired by a synthetic encounter with the text as a whole.

Several other problems, however, beyond that
of the mode of expression, confront the reader of
Chung-yung. These problems may be roughly divided
into problems of the general conceptualization of
the work and problems of its genesis. A major conceptual difficulty in approaching Chung-yung stems
from its "organismic" vision. The first chapter of
Chung-yung actually expounds the locus of all its
major concerns: the human way. Originated in Heav-
en and rooted in the nature of every person, the
human way is thought to have both metaphysical and
psychological significance. On the one hand, Chung-
yung asserts that human nature is imparted from
Heaven, thus affirming the ancient Chinese belief
in a purposive and caring Heaven as the ultimate
arbiter of human affairs. On the other, Chung-yung
also insists that teaching involves nothing but self-

realization and that it is through the understanding of things at hand that Heaven's true intentions are manifested, thus affirming another ancient Chinese belief that "man can make the Way great," but that "the Way cannot make man great."[5] The human way is therefore neither theocentric nor anthropocentric. Rather, it points to the mutuality of Heaven and man. By insisting upon a continuous interaction between them, the human way necessitates a transcendent anchorage for the existence of man and an immanent confirmation for the course of Heaven. Underlying this approach is perhaps the experience of what Eliade calls "anthropocosmic" unity,[6] the source of all the ethicoreligious symbolism in Chung-yung.

In the Judeo-Christian tradition, it is vitally important to recognize the ontological gap between Heaven and man. Man as a creature is fundamentally different from God as his ultimate reason for existence. To say that man, by self-effort, without a leap of faith,[7] can become one with the Creator is novel, if not, blasphemous, in the Judeo-Christian framework. It is true that one can emphasize the divine nature inherent in each human being, as differentiated from placing more weight on the notion of original sin,[8] but it remains extremely difficult to entertain the idea that self-knowledge is both the necessary and sufficient reason for

knowing the Christian God. Since the mode of thinking in Chung-yung is so radically different from the
predominant religious trend in the West, an appreciation of its spiritual orientation must be predicated on a willingness to suspend, at least for the
time being, judgments that may have been influenced
by the Judeo-Christian point of view.

Another difficulty lies in the relationship between Heaven and man, implicit in the human way in
Chung-yung itself. Professing the unity of man and
Heaven, Chung-yung neither denies nor slights a
transcendent reality.[9] Actually, since human nature
is imparted from and confirmed by Heaven, it is inconceivable in Chung-yung's view that man can be
alienated from Heaven in any essential way. As an
integral part of Heaven's creative process, man is
not only endowed with the "centrality" (the most refined quality) of the universe but is charged with
the mission of bringing the cosmic transformation
to its fruition. Therefore, the Way is nothing
other than the actualization of true human nature.
In a strict sense, the relationship between Heaven
and man is not that of creator and creature but one
of mutual fidelity;[10] and the only way for man to
know Heaven is to penetrate deeply into his own
ground of being. Consequently, any inquiry into
philosophy or religion must begin with a reflection
on the problem of man here and now.

The fact that Chung-yung takes man as its point of departure, however, does not necessarily commit it to the belief that "man is the measure of all things."[11] To be sure, one can argue that learning and teaching in Chung-yung are basically concerned with the problem of how to become a person, and that doctrines such as the unity of man and Heaven and the harmony of man and nature are manifestations of this humanistic concern. Spiritualism and naturalism as such do not play a key role in Chung-yung. But we would be ill-advised to interpret Chung-yung's humanism as a form of anthropocentrism, ignoring its spiritualist and naturalist dimensions.

Finally, we should note the difficulty resulting from what amounts to a serious cultural and historical gap in the understanding of what such a text as Chung-yung is and how it is to be read. The Confucian approach to classical literature in imperial China certainly differs from that of a modern student of Chinese intellectual history. For example, the time and energy allotted by an average educated person to the appreciation of Chung-yung in the Ming dynasty (1368-1644) is out of all proportion to what would seem appropriate to a doctoral candidate pursuing an advanced degree in Chinese thought in a modern university. The traditional Confucian student was likely to begin his study on Chung-yung as early as eight-years-old. He had time to grasp its meaning by being gradually steeped in it, after he had completely memorized the text. Without imposing a preconceived interpretive scheme upon it, he could try to realize its inner logic through personal knowledge. Systematic recitation, which is often misconstrued as unreasoning rote-learning, for him was intended to foster a holistic vision by a long and strenuous process of integrating the cognitive and experiential dimensions of his understanding of the text. Chu Hsi was absolutely serious when, in response to his students' queries about the expedient method of reading Confucian classics, he simply instructed them to experience the taste of it by "embodying" it in their daily lives.[12] Such advice must sound odd, if not totally irrational, to modern readers. We have neither the time nor the patience to internalize the text of Chung-yung; we are not even sure that it is really worth the effort. To many, whether its simplicity is deceptive or not, Chung-yung does seem short enough to be read, analyzed, and digested in a matter of days.

I do not presume to claim that the present study can overcome all of the conceptual difficulties of understanding Chung-yung just outlined. But my purpose is not to protect Chung-yung from misinterpretation, for I myself do not yet know how to arrive at a "correct" interpretation of the text.

I am acutely aware that a commitment to objectivity
is essential in any form of scholarly pursuit and
that there is, generally speaking, a major difference between an analytical inquiry and a personal
appreciation. The former is open to argument and
therefore allows for further investigation, whereas the latter all too often becomes an unyielding
fixity. My approach, however, is not a choice between these two modes but rather an attempt to com-
bine them. As with many other studies in religious
philosophy, the very fact that I have undertaken
the task of writing a systematic reflection of Chung-
yung already indicates a strong personal commitment
to it. And although this undertaking is predicated
in part on my belief that Chung-yung is one of the
most important texts in the Confucian tradition, it
also reflects the fact that this text has been exceedingly meaningful to me personally.

Apart from the conceptual difficulties just
discussed, another factor contributing to the relative neglect of Chung-yung in recent scholarship
is the cryptical nature of the text itself. A brief
survey of some of the genetic problems one is likely
to encounter in a systematic treatment of Chung-
yung therefore seems in order.

The first problem is that of authorship. As
is well known, this problem is common to virtually
all Confucian classics. The difficulty, however,

is not simply one of determining who composed a
specific text. The idea of a single author writing
a book at a given time is applicable only to a few
ancient Chinese texts. Most symbolize the cumulative efforts of scholars, involving masters, disciples, and followers of subsequent generations. A
text in this connection has a life history of its
own. In most cases it is extremely complicated, if
not impossible, to work out the genealogical tree
of a particular text. For example, the main body
of I Ching may have grown for centuries before it
became shaped into a relatively fixed form. Moreover, the true nature of the text is often further
confounded by commentators, interpreters, and, not
infrequently, interpolators.

Fortunately, the story of Chung-yung is less
exotic. Traditional scholars, including the classicist K'ung Ying-ta (574-648) and the philosopher
Chu Hsi (1130-1200), accepted the historian Ssu-ma
Ch'ien's (145-86 B.C.) account that Confucius'
grandson Tzu-ssu (492-431 B.C.) was the author.
Since the Ch'ing period (1644-1912), however, textual analysts have begun to question this; the majority believe that it was probably compiled during
the Warring States period (403-222 B.C.). Some
analysts have insisted that Chung-yung should be
dated around 200 B.C., after the Ch'in unification.[13]

Accordingly, several new theories have been

offered. Since the work first appeared as a chapter in the Book of Rites, compiled by Tai Sheng in
the Former Han dynasty (206 B.C.-8 A.D.), it has
been suggested that the author might have been Tai
himself,[14] but little textual evidence is available
to substantiate this claim. A more elaborate argument is that of the Ch'ing scholar Yü Cheng-hsieh
(1775-1840). He contends that after the burning
of the books by the first emperor of the Ch'in dynasty (221-206 B.C.), most classics had to be re-
constructed by scholars in the Han dynasty, and that
Chung-yung was no exception. The extant text, he
argues, was probably the result of the cooperative
effort of Han "doctorates" (po-shih) shortly after
the founding of the dynasty. Yü further suggests
that these doctorates must have consulted all the
available material on the subject, and that the underlying structure of the work therefore must be
basically in keeping with that of Tzu-ssu's original
text. Hence, he concludes, notwithstanding some
obvious evidence of later interpolation, Ssu-ma
Ch'ien was correct in assigning the authorship to
Tzu-ssu.[15] Scholars of a more critical bent, however, are not convinced that Tzu-ssu was the author
in the first place. The single reference in Ssu-ma
Ch'ien's Shih-chi (Record of history) is considered
insufficient. Such scholars believe that the text
was compiled by more than one person over a long

period of time and that it did not become "composed" until the early part of the Han dynasty. The well-known Ch'ing scholar, Ts'ui Shu (1740-1816), was an outstanding proponent of this position.[16]

A second difficulty centers on the historical problem of intellectual content. Chu Hsi was instrumental in bringing Chung-yung into prominence by selecting it, together with the Great Learning (another chapter from the Book of Rites), the Analects, and the Book of Mencius, to form the Four Books. From 1313 to 1905 the Four Books, as the basis for the civil service examinations, surpassed the Five Classics in exercising influence on the educated elite in imperial China. But even at the time when Pan Ku (32-92) compiled the first comprehensive bibliography of Chinese literature, Chung-yung had already come to be regarded as an independent treatise. The bibliographical essay on classical literature in the Sui dynasty (581-618) also includes a reference to Chung-yung as a work in itself. The founding emperor of the Liang dynasty, Wu-ti (464-549), is alleged to have personally written a commentary on it. His commentary is no longer extant, but it must have encouraged studies on Chung-yung in his court.[17]

According to one report, the Sung emperor Jen-tsung (1010-1063) once presented a copy of Chung-yung to his famous minister Wang Yao-ch'en (1001-

1056). The copy is said to have been done by the emperor himself in his own calligraphic style. For several decades after this, Chung-yung was frequently among the presents given by the emperor to successful candidates in the metropolitan examinations. Therefore, by early Sung (960-1279), it had already acquired a reputation as a major classic in the Confucian tradition.[18] The well-known story about Fan Chung-yen (989-1052), who instructed the youthful Chang Tsai (1020-1077) to study Chung-yung rather than military strategy, was probably not an isolated phenomenon.[19] Ssu-ma Kuang's (1019-1086) commentary on Chung-yung was a further indication of a new upsurge of interest in this short but extremely suggestive text.[20]

Thus, for more than a thousand years Chung-yung had received high acclaim as a vitally important legacy of the Confucian tradition. Its prestige was first brought into question by the philologists of the Ch'ing dynasty, notably Yuan Mei (1716-1797), Yeh Yü (b. 1739), and Yü Yüeh (1821-1906). Their queries were mainly directed to problems of authorship and dating.[21] Only very recently, however, have scholars begun to raise serious doubts about the intellectual content of Chung-yung. Ch'ien Mu, for example, has suggested that Chung-yung was deeply influenced by Taoist ideas and was in a sense composed in the spirit of Chuang Tzu.[22] Other interpreters tend to accept the thesis

that although Chung-yung is basically Confucian in
nature, it has been deeply influenced by Taoist
ideas. Some have pointed out that since Chung-yung
was enthusiastically commended by the two famous
monks, Chih-yuan (967-1022), who called himself
"Master Chung-yung," and Ch'i-sung (1007-1072), who
wrote a commentary on Chung-yung, its basic philosophical assumptions must be compatible with certain
schools of Buddhism. The question of how Taoistic
or Buddhistic Chung-yung is has therefore become a
prominent concern for students of Chinese thought.[23]

A third difficulty involves the organization
of Chung-yung. In terms of length, Chung-yung is
certainly one of the shortest classics in the Confucian canon. In all, the main text contains 3,544
Chinese characters.[24] Traditionally, according to
Cheng Hsüan's (127-200) Li-chi cheng-i (Correct
meanings of the Book of Rites), it is divided into
two parts and thirty-six sections. With some minor
alterations of the order of the text, Chu Hsi re-
divided the text into thirty-three sections. Other
attempts have included the division into eighty-two
sections by the Sung scholar Chao Yueh-chih (1059-
1129), the division into twelve sections by the
Ch'ing scholar Li Kuang-ti (1642-1718), and a number
of variations in between.[25]

Actually, the practice of sectioning the text
in this way only scratches the surface of the or-

ganizational problem. Chung-yung, like the Analects and the Great Learning, is stylistically highly condensed. And since its aphoristic formulations are deceptively simple, one can be easily led to believe that the text consists of many loosely connected statements and falls short of a systematic coherence. Indeed, if one is looking for an argument with a linear unfolding of rationally constructed propositions, the structure of Chung-yung must appear hopelessly confusing, and it becomes tempting to reorganize the text according to a set of preconceived criteria in order to make the material lucid to the analytical mind. The danger of imposing an alien structure upon Chung-yung in the name of persuasive rationality and so creating all sorts of misconceptions is acute. Yet, unless one wishes to avoid making any broad interpretive commitments and to confine one's efforts to philological and textual matters, a certain degree of generalization, bordering perhaps on imposition, may be inevitable.

Yet another methodological difficulty that one encounters in a study of Chung-yung is that of terminology. One of the major problems in writing about Chung-yung, or about any other Confucian classic, in a non-ideogrammatic language, is that the associational meanings and the fruitful nuances of the concrete symbol have to be sacrificed. This is further complicated by the fact that some of the

key concepts in <u>Chung-yung</u> have particular connotations that are unusual even to those who are
versed in classical Chinese. Clearly, problems of
this kind cannot be solved by focusing exclusively
on literal accuracy. Unless we also take readabil-
ity into consideration, translation of key terms is
bound to be clumsy and even incomprehensible.

To avoid terminological ambiguity, all that we
can try to achieve is a contextual approximation to
the original. The appearance of the same term in
different contexts should provide sufficient ground
to cover the missing ramifications of the original
idea. For example, the term <u>chün-tzu</u> will be rendered as the "profound person."[26] It is hoped that
our discussions on the profound person will provide
an intellectual framework in which the political,
the social, the moral, and the religious dimensions
of the personality ideal will all be accommodated.
On the other hand, the term <u>ch'eng</u>, which has been
somewhat unjustifiably translated as "sincerity,"
will often remain in its romanized form. The complexities of this key concept, however, may be better appreciated if, through both textual and philosophical analyses, <u>ch'eng</u> can be shown to connote
meanings such as "genuineness," "truthfulness," and
"reality" as well as the commonly used notion of
"sincerity."[27]

The final methodological problem to be considered here is the title of the text. Chung-yung

has been translated as "The Doctrine of the Mean"

by James Legge, "The Mean-in-Action" by E. R. Hughes,

"Central Harmony" by the classicist Ku Hung-ming,

and "The Unwobbling Pivot" by Ezra Pound.[28] Al-

though the term chung can be rendered as "central-

ity" without causing much controversy, the concept

of yung raises many puzzling questions.[29] In one

of its earliest commentaries, yung is defined by

Ch'eng Hsüan as "practice." Chung-yung thus means

"the practical application of the principle of cen-

tral harmony."[30] Ch'eng I (1033-1107), one of the

most perceptive thinkers in the Sung dynasty, said,

"By chung is meant what is not one-sided, and by

yung is meant what is unchangeable. Chung is the

correct path of the world and yung is the definite

principle of the world."[31] Ch'eng's disciple Kuo

Chung-hsiao further stated that "chung is the ulti-

mate realization of that which is absolutely rec-

tifying in the world, and yung is the comprehensive

penetration of that which is absolutely transforming

in the world."[32] Chu Hsi, however, after systemat-

ically studying virtually all available interpreta-

tions, concluded that yung signifies that which is

"ordinary" and "common."[33] It should become clear

in the course of our discussion that yung, which we

will translate as "commonality," must be taken as

including such connotations as "practicality" and

"unchangeability."[34]

Having noted some of the problems that must be confronted in any analytical study of Chung-yung, I should state my own methodological preferences. On the issue of authorship, I tend to accept the view that the text was not composed by a single author for a definite purpose but is the result of a cumulative effort of many scholars over a long stretch of time. The claim that Chung-yung is probably of composite authorship can be substantiated by the fact that, in terms of its content, the text can be divided into three distinct parts: the first nineteen chapters deal mainly with the character and duties of the chün-tzu (gentleman, superior man, and in this study "profound person"); the twentieth chapter, especially its first fifteen sections, deals mainly with the idea of cheng (politics), including the moral responsibilities and the ideal institutions of the sage-kings; and the last thirteen chapters deal mainly with the metaphysical concept of ch'eng (sincerity, reality, and truth). However, although I am not convinced that one of its authors was indeed the grandson of Confucius, Tzu-ssu (K'ung Chi, 491-431 B.C.); I would assume that the work was written in the school of Tzu-ssu and therefore is compatible in spirit with the Mencian tradition.[35] Of course, by accepting Chung-yung as a work in the school of Tzu-ssu, I do not suggest that it necessarily predates the Book of Mencius. I would only maintain that the text as a whole is a coherent statement about humanity rather than a collection of unrelated proverbs. Therefore, my position is that, notwithstanding its composite authorship, Chung-yung can be analyzed as an integrated series of reflections on personality, society, and metaphysics.

On the issue of the intellectual content, my choice is relatively simple. Although Ch'ien Mu's systematic attempt to underscore the importance of what he believes to be the Taoist element in Chung-yung clearly shows that there are points of resonance between Chung-yung and the philosophy of Chuang Tzu, his assertion that Chung-yung was, in fact, a Taoist text in the tradition of Chuang Tzu is still too controversial to be taken as a sound historical judgment. In Hsü Fu-kuan's critique of Ch'ien's claim, at least seven pieces of textual evidence are identified to show that Chung-yung is closely linked with the Analects.[36] In a similar critique, Huang Chang-chien points out that an entire chapter in Chung-yung is virtually identical to a passage in the Book of Mencius.[37] Ch'en P'an further advances the thesis that Chung-yung is basically a Confucian text of the pre-Ch'in period.[38] The contention that it might have been influenced by early Taoist literature or that it might have ex-

erted influence upon Taoism and Buddhism in subsequent years is not in conflict with the belief that
Chung-yung is a vitally important part of classical
Confucian legacy. Indeed, it can be further suggested that without Chung-yung, our conceptions of
classical Confucianism would need to be reformulated.
However, by assuming that Chung-yung is basically
Confucian, I do not necessarily subscribe to a given
interpretation of what Confucianism ought to be. My
study on Chung-yung may help to open up the range
and mode of inquiry into that subject.

On the organizational problem, there is no
simple choice to make. If my study is to be meaningful not only to specialists in the field but also
to students of religious philosophy in general, the
proposal of a certain overall structure is inevitable. However, resisting the temptation to tie up
loose ends prematurely, I propose that the structure
be flexible enough to accommodate the bulk of the
available material. Of course, the purpose of my
study is not to present a comprehensive cataloguing
of primary sources. But the practice of abstracting
a few concepts from their complicated interconnec-
tions in order to focus on a limited number of issues is equally unfruitful, for a classic of the
first rank must be assumed to have an inner logic
of its own. And if this is so, no holistic vision
of it can ever be cultivated by treating selected

concepts in isolation.

My approach, then, is to identify three mutually complementary problem areas for investigation: profound person, fiduciary community, and moral metaphysics. These three topics are broad enough to include virtually all material in the text and yet as analytical categories do not function merely as classificatory schemes. It is hoped that a series of disciplined reflections on the key concepts relating to these three fields of inquiry will evoke a sense of the interconnectedness of the text, and as a result disclose, as it were, the "internal structure" of Chung-yung. To borrow from Tseng Tzu, the task is like "standing on the brink of a deep abyss and treading on thin ice."[39] One can easily suffer from shipwreck on either the Scylla of reading too much into it or the Charybdis of leaving too much of it unsaid.

This chapter began with an examination of the conceptual difficulty that the organismic vision of Chung-yung presents to the reader. Inasmuch as the first chapter of Chung-yung provides us with a key to the holistic structure of the text, we return to it now from a different perspective, focusing on the unfolding of the organismic vision. In order to understand the meaning of this vision, we must first discuss what Chung-yung's human way really entails.

The human way as the Way of the profound person is, on the one hand, deeply rooted in the nature conferred by Heaven, and on the other, universally manifested in the daily affairs of the world. Thus the Way has both a central focus and a general application. The central focus is not a spatial concept; it is that which ontologically defines what a person is. This centrality signifies the most refined and absolutely irreducible quality inherent in each human being. To be sure, this concept resembles the idea of the unchangeable essence, but it is not merely an abstract notion. The essence of human beings, in this connection, is more than a logical postulate; it is an experienced reality. Therefore, the Way issuing from the center "cannot be separated from us for a moment." And we know that which "can be separated from us is not the Way." The transcendental truth, devoid of any human content, is certainly not the Way of Chung-yung. The idea of an afterlife that has nothing to do with the human condition in the lived world and the path that eventually leads to the denial of humanity are in sharp conflict with Chung-yung's philosophical intent.

It is not surprising that the profound person is "cautious over what he does not see and apprehensive over what he does not hear." Indeed, his central concern is not the external object that can be grasped by outwardly projecting his sense perceptions, but the sightless and soundless processes of the inner self. Since he is absolutely serious about the quality of his being, as it manifests itself in the innermost sphere of feelings and thoughts, he is extremely attentive to the real world within. His caution and apprehension, in a primary sense, have little to do with pressures from outside. He is cautious or apprehensive not over any particular thing but over the entire spectrum of his existence. That which he sees and hears as reflected manifestations of his way of life is vitally important to him, but he is more concerned about the hidden and subtle workings of his inner self that have originally evoked such responses. For the profound person, self-knowledge is a prerequisite for a fruitful encounter with the external world. Therefore, "the true student learns for the sake of himself, whereas the vulgarized scholar learns for the sake of others."[40] It is in this connection that the "hidden" and "subtle" indications of the internal world are to him the most visible and manifested realities of life. He is "watchful over himself when he is alone" because he cares not only about the consequences of his action but also about the motivational structure behind it.

Centrality, then, is that state of mind wherein one is absolutely unperturbed by outside forces. But it is more than a psychological concept of equilibrium since it is not so much an achieved ideal as a given reality. According to an ancient tradition, certainly antedating the composition of Chung-yung, man is conceived as that being which embodies the centrality of heaven and earth. Accordingly, it is by the centrality inherent in each human being that man becomes united with heaven and earth. In a strict sense, centrality signifies an ontological condition rather than a mental state of quiescence. And it is only to that inner self, "before the feelings of pleasure, anger, sorrow, and joy are aroused," that the term centrality can be adequately applied. Ontologically, since the aroused feelings are manifestations of centrality, it is natural that they "each and all attain due measure and degree." Harmony so conceived is necessarily a mirror image of centrality. It is in this connection that centrality is thought to be the ultimate ground of existence: "the great foundation of the world," and harmony its unfolding process of self-expression: "its universal path."

Although the great foundation of the world is inherent in each person, there is no guarantee that one will actualize it in a harmonious state of existence. There is, in a practical sense, a major difference between what one is and what one can become. It should be noted that since this kind of gap is different from that between God as the Creator and man as a creature in Christian theology, the moral and social ramifications it entails are also dissimilar to those in Christian ethics. In the case of Chung-yung, the attempt to bridge the gap takes the form of self-cultivation. The ultimate source of legitimacy as well as the energy necessary for undertaking the task is thought to be internally based. There is no need for asceticism and there is no conception of transcendent grace. Yet the burden is heavy and the road long; it requires a total commitment no less intensive than the bearing of the cross. "To cultivate centrality and harmony with thoroughness" is therefore an unceasing process of learning. Since such a process is intended to realize the centrality of the universe in concrete human affairs so that a state of harmony among the myriad things can be attained, the highest ideal is the synchronicity of heaven and earth and the symbiosis between different modes of existence. The discussions that follow on the profound person, the fiduciary community, and the moral metaphysics are three interconnected ways of expounding this basic insight of Chung-yung.

CHAPTER 2

THE PROFOUND PERSON

The profound person in <u>Chung-yung</u> seeks to
manifest the ultimate meaning of ordinary human
existence. This is predicated on the belief that
the most generalized level of universality (Heaven)
is rooted in concrete and specific acts in the
everyday lives of human beings. The profound person
recognizes that the possibility of a complete realization of the ideal of the unity of man and Heaven
is inherent in each human nature. He also recognizes
that, despite great differences in intelligence,
talent, and ability, all human beings are endowed
with the inner strength to actualize themselves so
that they can reach the fullest state of identification with the cosmos.

A defining characteristic of the profound person is his faith in humanity. We are told that the
human way is near at hand and that the mode of pursuing it is easy and simple. In fact, all we need
to do is to be "watchful over ourselves when we are
alone." It would appear that the human way involves no more than an ordinary process of self-
education. And <u>Chung-yung</u> makes it explicit that
the profound person's knowledge of the Way is shared

and practiced by men and women of simple intelligence
as well [XII:1-2]. After all, the way of the profound person is also the way of the commoner.
Throughout Chung-yung, imagery of common activities
such as eating and walking is employed to describe
the Way. Time and again, Chung-yung stresses that
no external help is essential to the actualization
of one's own human way [I:2, XIII:1, XIV:5, XX:1-2].
To become a profound person is accordingly to be
truthful to oneself. What is there to be learned,
if we are asked to become no more and no less than
ourselves?

To be sure, the way of the profound person is
compatible with such familiar acts as eating and
walking; it is not separable from daily affairs.
However, to eat and to be able to know the real
taste of the food or to walk in order to arrive at
the journey's end is no easy task. It is not difficult to eat right occasionally or to make progress
toward one's destination once in a while. But the
profound person manifests the principle of centrality[1]--the human way--in an unceasing process of self-
realization. He always acts in accordance with the
principle. Despite the fact that all people can follow the human way, the majority fail to do so most
of the time. The profound person, in contrast, maintains his humanity all the time, though by nature
he is not at all different from a common person.

Yet it is misleading to suggest that the profound person differs from a common person only in
degree but never in kind. The ability to manifest
the human way as an integral part of one's daily
existence connotes a qualitative refinement of the
conditions of life that can hardly be measured in
quantitative terms. This does not imply that the
profound person, as contrasted with an ordinary human being, is a different sort of being altogether.
It could, of course, be argued that the profound
person has little in common with an ordinary human
being, and that even his ways of eating and walking
must be interpreted in terms of an entirely different structure of meaning. But Chung-yung insists
that since the point of departure remains the same,
the profound person is by necessity a man among men.

The discussion thus far may give rise to some
confusion: What is a profound person really? If
he is significantly different from us, why can he
not be defined as an entirely different sort of
being? If he is, like us, bewilderingly human, why
are we tempted to feel that he should be appreciated
in an entirely different structure of meaning? The
difficulty in part lies in Chung-yung's language itself. Without any argumentative explanation, it
tells us both that the profound person (1) simply
realizes his nature as a human being, and (2)
achieves a level of existence no ordinary mortal,

not even Yen Hui, the most admired disciple of Confucius, can actually attain. One way to approach
this problem is to keep the apparent incompatibility
in mind while focusing on the assumptive reasoning
in Chung-yung.

That Chung-yung depicts the way of the profound
person as common to every human being and yet as
uniquely manifested by sage-kings such as Great Shun,
without even acknowledging the theoretical complexity of maintaining such an interpretation, seems to
indicate a matter-of-fact attitude toward problems
of this kind. The question of why the way of the
profound person, despite its universality and commonality, can only be actualized in unique personalities
is never fully answered. The available sources,
which can serve as a kind of implicit explanation,
frequently lead the reader to a deceptively simple
solution: since the profound person is endowed with
the same human nature as men and women of simple intelligence, every human being can become a profound
person; the fact that there are not many profound
persons in a given society merely signifies that only a few have the inner strength to fully actualize
that which is inherent in them.

One way of perceiving the profound person,
then, is to characterize him in terms of a process
toward an ever-deepening subjectivity. To be "cautious over what he does not see" and "apprehensive

over what he does not hear" is a conscious attempt
to look and listen for subtle manifestations of his
inner self so that he can fully actualize the human
way inherent in his nature. Although this particular concern is never private, it can hardly be recognized by a set of behavioral criteria. To be
sure, the quality of one's life will somehow makes
its appearance in an observable pattern of conduct.
And, despite the uncertainty of one's public image,
one frequently learns about oneself through the
"eyes" and "ears" of other people. Self-knowledge,
to a large measure, depends upon an appreciation of
the responses of others to one's varied modes of
existence. The profound person is therefore certainly not insensitive to critical judgments from
outside. Nevertheless, he is more attentive to a
comprehensive and unceasing process of internal examination. It is, to be sure, misleading to suggest
that his self-confidence makes him less concerned
about the opinions of others than about his own feelings. The profound person is indeed mindful of his
reputation, but in order to make it compatible with
his self-definition at any given time, he must not
only have the courage to resist the temptation of
premature recognition but also the strength to carry
on a long and strenuous task of self-cultivation at
his own pace. It is only when he has focused his
attention on the depth of his subjectivity that he

becomes "watchful over himself when he is alone."

"Self-watchfulness when alone" (shen-tu) may simply suggest a kind of unremitting vigilance. A person who watches over himself when alone is also likely to be sensitive to the external environment, to be aware of situations around him, and to be alert in confronting unexpected developments. This sensitivity, awareness, and alertness enables him to apprehend with ready promptness that which "he does not see and does not hear" under ordinary circumstances. The self-watchful person is not necessarily a clairvoyant, but his personal knowledge is such that he can fully comprehend matters beyond the range of normal perception. His ability to have such clear-sightedness is not because he is by chance endowed with some unusual power of apprehension. Rather, it is through his continuous effort of critical self-examination that he becomes perceptive of the subtle manifestation of his inner feelings.

Since a person in the Confucian tradition is always conceived of as a center of relationships, it is believed that the more one penetrates into one's inner self, the more one will be capable of realizing the true nature of one's human-relatedness. Accordingly, "self-watchfulness when alone," as a spiritual cultivation, far from being a quest for the idiosyncrasy of an atomized individual, is intended to reach levels of that reality which underlies common human-

ity. The profound person does not practice self-
watchfulness for the intrinsic value of being alone.
In fact, he sees little significance in solitari-
ness, unless it is totally integrated into the
structure of social relations.

Yet the profound person's process toward an
ever-deepening subjectivity is not determined by
any external motivation, whether it is religiously
sanctioned or socially conditioned. It is not a
process of internalization in the psychological sense
either. What Chung-yung envisions seems to be a
creative process of self-realization, fostered by
a self-generating source of strength. Strictly
speaking, one cannot become a profound person by
model learning. Unless one has already come to
terms with one's inner self, that which is hidden
and subtle to others but visible and manifest to oneself, modeling one's life upon an established pattern of behavior will be a limited and limiting experience.[2] Indeed, Confucius said, "In archery we
have something resembling the Way of the profound
person. When the archer misses the center of the
target, he turns around and seeks for the cause of
failure within himself" [XIV:5]. By quoting this
passage, Chung-yung intends to illustrate that the
centeredness of one's existence in a complicated
nexus of human-relatedness is predicated upon one's
ability to be "at ease with oneself."

Needless to say, being "at ease with oneself" is not merely a demonstration of self-control. The ability to control one's emotions and to act with self-restraint in hostile situations is an obvious but rather superficial aspect of the way of the profound person. What he really excels in is not passive adjustment but creative transformation. While ordinary people are all capable of acting in accordance with the principle of centrality sometimes, the profound person embodies the principle in his daily life to the extent that he can always feel "at ease with himself." Chung-yung states:

> The profound person does what is proper to his position and does not want to go beyond this. If he is in a noble station, he does what is proper to a position of wealth and honorable station. If he is in a humble station, he does what is proper to a position of poverty and humble station. If he is in the midst of barbarian tribes, he does what is proper in the midst of barbarian tribes. In a position of difficulty and danger, he does what is proper to a position of difficulty and danger. [XIV:1-2]

The first reading of this passage may give one the impression that the profound person responds to the challenges of his environment in a compromising mood, and thus presents a clear example of situation-

al ethics at work. To be sure, the conscious attempt of the profound person to harmonize himself
with his environment necessarily involves situation-
al choices. He cannot afford to be an isolated individual. But the real strength of the profound
person lies not so much in his adaptability as in
his self-identity. Indeed, his ability to bring
himself into harmony with an alienating environment
is a demonstration of his self-knowledge as well as
an indication of his pragmatism. If he always knows
where he stands in relationship to a constantly
changing structure of human-relatedness, this is because, far from simply performing a function in the
social hierarchy, he realizes his moral principles
in spite of it: "In a high position he does not
treat his inferiors with contempt, and in a low position he does not court the favor of his superiors."
[XIV:3].

Being situated in a complex structure of dyadic
relationships is certainly constraining. It is no
easy task to do justice to them all. In Chung-yung,
Confucius is alleged to have said:

There are four things in the way of the
profound man, none of which I have been able
to do. To serve my father as I would expect
my son to serve me: that I have not been
able to do. To serve my ruler as I would
expect my ministers to serve me: that I

have not been able to do. To serve my elder
brothers as I would expect my younger brothers to serve me: that I have not been able
to do. To be the first to treat friends as
I would expect them to treat me: that I
have not been able to do. In practicing the
ordinary virtues and in the exercise of care
in ordinary conversation, when there is de-
ficiency, the profound person never fails to
make further effort, and when there is excess,
never dares to go to the limit. His words
correspond to his action and his actions
correspond to his words. The profound person
is indeed earnest and genuine. [XIII:4]

It would appear that, lurking behind what one com-
mentator characterizes as Confucius' pedagogical de-
vice of self-criticism,[3] is his acute awareness of
the difficulty of assuming common roles, such as the
son, the minister, the younger brother, and the
friend. By the same token, it is equally demanding
to assume the role of father, ruler, or elder brother. In light of this, the profound person is at ease
with himself wherever he dwells, not because he is
particularly fortunate in his social dealings but because he "rectifies himself and seeks nothing from
others" [XIV:3]. Although the profound person is
never self-centered or conceited, his inner strength
helps him to recognize the creative possibilities of
his own lot, no matter what it happens to be: "Hence
he has no complaint to make. He does not complain

against Heaven above or blame men below" [XIV:3].

This may seem to be an unmitigated form of
self-sufficiency. But the way of the profound person is predicated on a continuous encounter with the
other. It is inconceivable that he would willfully
withdraw from society for the sake of spiritual purity. To say that "he seeks nothing from others" is
not to suggest that he secludes himself from others.
On the contrary, it is precisely because of his dis-
interestedness in social relations that he is capable of entering into meaningful associations with
others. His self-rectification, as a result, is
instrumental in bringing about a more amicable environment for himself and for those around him. Probably it is in this sense that Chung-yung states that
"the profound person lives peacefully and at ease and
waits for his destiny, while the shallow man takes to
dangerous courses and hopes for good luck" [XIV:4].

The concept of "waiting for his destiny" needs
some explanation. The Chinese term ming, in its ordinary usage, certainly connotes the predetermined
course of events, and is often conceived as the irresistible function of a hidden and mysterious agent.
It can thus be rendered also as "fate." However,
the Confucian idea of ming is so laden with ethicoreligious implications that it is inadequate to define it simply in terms of a law of necessity.[4] In
the context of Chung-yung, to wait for one's ming

strongly suggests the fulfillment of one's human way. It is vitally important to note that ming in this sense specifically refers to the Mandate of Heaven. Since human nature is what Heaven "imparts" (ming), to wait for the Mandate of Heaven is not merely to meet an irrevocable appointment but to be met by natural fulfillment. Indeed, the courage and wisdom of "waiting" rather than of anticipating is set in sharp contradistinction to the restless attempts of the shallow man to impose his self-centeredness upon the existing constellation of affairs. I must hasten to point out that the profound person, far from adjusting passively to the status quo, seeks to transform the world in the spirit of chung-yung, for he believes that the "middle" path is also the most universal and practical way.

It may well be argued that the uniqueness of the profound person lies not so much in the structure of his way as in how he integrates it with his life. It is not a question of form or content, nor is it the problem of choosing between two fundamentally different modes of existence. People are all capable of pursuing the way of the profound person. There is nothing in their original human constitution that prevents them from doing so. Actually, as we have already pointed out, the way of the profound person is what is also manifested in the daily lives of ordinary men and women without their being aware

of it. After all, "the way of the profound person
may be compared to travelling to a distant place:
one must start from the nearest point. It may be
compared to ascending a height: one must start from
below" [XV:1]. Accordingly, without stretching the
definition, the way of the profound person can even
be understood as the "common" way. To become a profound person is not to "seek for the abstruse, and
practice wonders" [XI:1], but to achieve what the
Book of Odes extols: "Happy union with wife and
children is like the music of lutes and harps. When
brothers live in concord and at peace, the harmony is
sweet and delightful. Let your family live in concord, and enjoy your wife and children" [XV:2].

Yet to follow the common way and to become an
integral part of it requires a lifelong commitment.
To be sure, the kinds of things to be performed are
obvious; they all derive from common sense. Underlying this apparent simplicity, however, is a pervasive and powerful demand for consistency. That is
the rub. We can certainly follow the principle of
centrality to a degree, but to be like Yen Hui, who
attempted to "clasp it firmly as if wearing it on
his breast and never to lose it" [VIII], is an entirely different matter. There is no simple explanation for the fact that only a very few can follow the
Way in a continuous manner. Confucius made an observation:

> I know why the Way is not pursued. The
> intelligent go beyond it and the unintelli-
> gent do not come up to it. I know why the
> Way is not understood. The worthy go beyond
> it and the unworthy do not come up to it.
> There is no one who does not eat and drink,
> but there are few who can really know flavor.
> [IV:1-2]

To paraphrase a statement in Chung-yung, we all think
that we know what we want; but when driven forward
and taken in a net, a trap, or a pitfall, none knows
how to escape. Similarly, we all think that we know
what we can do; but should we choose the way of the
profound person, we are probably not able to keep it
for a round month [VII].

The real problem, then, is our inability to
know the Way to the extent that we can have an experiential understanding of its true "taste." This
is one of the basic reasons why, despite its commonness, the Way cannot be completely realized in our
lives. There are, of course, other equally distress-
ing difficulties. For one thing, the Way can never
be specified in terms of objective doctrines. It is
absolutely impossible to establish a fixed model by
which all people can learn to become profound persons. The Way can neither be determined by a limited
set of rules nor be divided into discrete stages in a
unilinear procedure. The multiplicity of models as
well as the complexity of rules and procedures ren-

ders it unrealistic even to attempt the formulation
of an all-embracing pattern of behavior universally
applicable to those aspiring to become profound persons. The following statement from Chung-yung is
particularly pertinent:

> The way of the profound person functions
> everywhere and yet is hidden. Men and women
> of simple intelligence can share its knowledge;
> and yet in its utmost reaches, there is some-
> thing which even the sage does not know. Men
> and women of simple intelligence can put it
> into practice; and yet in its utmost reaches
> there is something which even the sage is not
> able to put into practice. [XII:1-2]

Inasmuch as the Way functions everywhere, it is common; but, since it is not a static fixity but a dynamic process, its meaning can never be fully compre-
hended and its potential never exhausted. There is
always something "hidden," so to speak, in its commonness.

Certainly, the fact that the way of the profound person can, on the one hand, be manifested in
the lives of ordinary people and, on the other, be
hidden from the sages is verifiable by common experience. We all, to a certain extent, practice the
ordinary virtues of serving our parents, taking care
of our children, or helping our friends. Few do all
these things regularly and conscientiously. Still

fewer try to integrate their daily lives with their quests for self-knowledge. It is indeed rare to find those who act to establish long-lasting values by giving a general structure of meaning to their everyday activities. And it is almost impossible to imagine that a single person, by a strenuous process of self-realization in the context of ordinary human-relatedness, can creatively transform the existing world and formulate an ultimate order of existence which is powerful and pervasive enough to become a defining characteristic of human heritage.

Similarly, despite the near impossibility of our approximating what the sage can do, we can still understand that even his great accomplishments do not exhaust all the subtleties of practicing ordinary virtues such as serving parents, taking care of children, and helping friends. There is always room for self-cultivation in every human being, including the most profound person, the sage. Understandably, there are so-called profound persons who "act in accordance with the Way, but give it up when they have gone half way" [XI:2]. And it takes no less than a sage to totally commit himself to the principle of centrality, even though throughout his life his efforts are never recognized. Confucius was absolutely serious when he said that "the empire, the states, and the families can be put in order. Ranks and emolument can be declined. A bare, naked weapon can be tramped upon. But the principle of centrality cannot be attained" [IX].

Of course, to say that the principle of centrality cannot be attained does not mean that it has never been observed. Such a concept does suggest, however, that the complete actualization of the principle of centrality, which is tantamount to the full realization of the way of the profound person, is more challenging than the greatest display of political skill and the boldest demonstration of physical courage. It is in this connection that Confucius stressed the importance of having sufficient strength to sustain the task of becoming a profound person. However, Confucius further suggested that, unlike the strength of the people of the North, which is "to lie under arms and meet death without regret," the kind of strength that the profound person cultivates is comparable to the strength of the people of the South: "to be genial and gentle in teaching others and not to revenge unreasonable conduct" [X:1-4]. Therefore, the profound person is not only a sensitive man who is always at ease with himself, but a courageous man:

> The profound person maintains harmony
> [in his nature and conduct] and does not
> waver. How unflinching is his strength!
> He stands in the middle position and does
> not lean to one side. How unflinching is

his strength! When the Way prevails in the
state, [if he enters public life], he does
not change from what he was in private life.
How unflinching is his strength! When the
Way does not prevail in the state, he does
not change even unto death. How unflinching
is his strength! [X:5]

We have already pointed out that the profound
person is watchful over himself when he is alone; he
is conscientious about not only the observable patterns of his behavior, but also the incipient tenden-
cies of his inner feelings. He is honest with himself in the sense that he is truthful to his genuine
self. This requires a great deal of courage: to
cultivate the mental willingness necessary to endure
the hardship of self-examination. We have also mentioned that the profound person is a man among men
and thus mindful of human relationships. He is never
an isolated individual, nor does he by conscious
choice refrain from involvement in the affairs of the
world. Indeed, he is so much concerned about the
welfare of the people that, even though he is realis-
tically aware of his own limitations, he resists the
temptation to forsake his sociopolitical responsibility: "I know that it cannot be done; yet I cannot
but do it."[5] This also requires a great deal of
courage: to confront the danger of being torn apart
by dehumanizing forces from outside. The profound

person is therefore honest with himself and considerate toward others. Since conscientiousness and altruism are means of actualizing the Way,[6] the Confucian golden rule reads: "What you do not wish others to do to you, do not do to them."[7]

The underlying argument is not difficult to see, but some explanatory notes are in order. Heuristically, the Way of the profound person can be conceived in terms of two interrelated dimensions--conscientiousness (chung) within and altruism (shu) without. To be conscientious is to be utterly serious about one's internal self-cultivation. This entails an unceasing attempt to delve deeply, as it were, into the bedrock of one's existence. The intention is to come to terms with all the weaknesses one has, such as an inertial resistance to new environments and an unobserving tendency to limit one's creative potential. The former makes one ill at ease in new situations and the latter may gradually numb one's sensibility toward self-improvement, which is described in Confucian literature as drawing a line to restrict one's possibility of moral growth.[8] Having acquired a new level of self-awareness, the conscientious person continues to cultivate his inner sensibility so that his feelings, no matter how subtle they are, can always manifest the centeredness of his inner self in a state of harmony.

The conscientiousness of the profound person

toward himself, however, is not in conflict with his
concern for others. Being altruistic, he is neither
compulsive nor demanding. In his intercourse with
people, he is not opinionated; he listens well to
others' suggestions. He is not absolute in carrying
out his ideas; he appreciates the limitation of his
own perceptions. He is not stubborn, for he sees
flexibility as a positive virtue for opening up new
possibilities in human understanding. And he is never self-centered, for he defines his existence in
terms of human-relatedness.[9] On the surface, he is
open-minded, accommodating, flexible, and considerate
because he is mindful of his social relations. Upon
reflection, however, his concern for his encounters
with others is actually predicated upon a deeper concern for the integrities of those who have entered
into relationship with him. To impose upon them a
structure of values that has no roots in their nature
would be diametrically opposed to his belief that inner sensibility is the basis of self-improvement.[10]
There is no compelling reason why he must dictate
rules for them to follow. If they have no intention
of pursuing the Way, coercive rules are virtually
useless. What he can and should do is to set an example and to exert his moral influence through exemplary teaching. Even then his function is not to
command but to show, to suggest, and indeed, like
Confucius, to "lure."[11]

There are great complexities involved in the relationship between conscientiousness and altruism in the way of the profound person, and many of them have far-reaching philosophical implications that cannot be easily unraveled in this monograph. It is perhaps useful to point out that the seeming lack of assertiveness in the profound person's instructions to others, as contrasted with his strong demand for self-cultivation, is not dictated by a sense of politeness. The issue of etiquette is only marginally relevant in this connection. The profound person certainly intends to share his inner experiences, for he is confident that what he really cherishes, such as the ordinary virtues just mentioned is of immense value to others as well. Moreover, since he has absolute faith in the perfectibility of human nature through self-effort, he strongly believes that what he himself cultivates in moral situations can be commonly practiced by his fellow human beings. And it is precisely in this sense that he never pontificates; nor does he assume the role of an accomplished master. His self-image, even in reference to his fellow students, is basically one of a "traveler" on the Way. It is only because he cannot be sure of the situations of others in the same way and to the same degree as his own that he is reluctant to pass judgment on them.

The profound person has no transcendent ref-

erence to rely upon, thus cannot be absolutely sure
whether that which is best for him is necessarily of
equal value to others. Although he envisages his own
quest for his inner self as a universal path, he does
not presume to have a privileged access to esoteric
truths. Rather, he addresses himself to common phenomena and points out to others what they themselves
are capable of learning and knowing. He reflects on
things at hand with the intention of establishing
himself so that others can also be established.[12]
To be sure, he hopes that his fellow human beings will
all appreciate what he believes to be true and valuable, but he has no compulsion to see to it that his
"world view" is universally accepted. His duty is to
rectify himself and to help others to rectify themselves. To reiterate an earlier point, since "he
seeks nothing from others, he has no complaint to
make" [XIV:3]. As he conscientiously attends to his
own affairs and altruistically sympathizes with the
feelings of others, he cultivates a courage to probe
all layers of his inner self and a sensitivity "not
to do to others, what he does not wish others to do
to him."[13]

Thus far the profound person has been primarily
portrayed as a person who has a profound concern for
common sense. It might not be wide of the mark to
conclude that the profound person seeks to enact the
ultimate meaning of life in ordinary human existence.

And <u>Chung-yung</u> maintains that the applicability of
such a simple observation is unlimited and its implications inexhaustible:

> Great as heaven and earth are, men still
> find something in them with which to be dis-
> satisfied. Thus with [the Way of] the pro-
> found person, if one speaks of its greatness,
> nothing in the world can contain it, and if
> one speaks of its smallness, nothing in the
> world can split it. The <u>Book of Odes</u> says,
> "the hawk flies up to heaven; the fishes leap
> in the deep." This means that [the Way] is
> clearly seen above and below. The Way of the
> profound person has its simple beginnings
> among ordinary men and women, but in its ut-
> most reaches, it is clearly seen in heaven
> and on earth. [XII:2-4]

CHAPTER 3

THE FIDUCIARY COMMUNITY

If the profound person seeks to manifest the
ultimate meaning of ordinary human existence, he
cannot afford to slight interpersonal relationships.
To say that the way of the profound person has its
simple beginnings in the lives of ordinary men and
women implies that human-relatedness is, in fact,
its point of departure. This is in perfect accord
with the fact that the Confucian tradition has always stressed the significance of sociality. But
is this emphasis on human-relatedness at all compatible with Chung-yung's insistence that self-cultivation necessarily involves a process of inner moral
and spiritual transformation? Indeed, it would seem
to be in an apparent conflict with the perception
that the profound person is engaged in an ever-
deepening process toward subjectivity.

Beyond doubt, a unique feature of Chung-yung's
thinking is its focus on the profound person's quest
for self-realization. Phrases such as "watchfulness
in solitude" and "subtle manifestations" further suggest that the work puts much emphasis on the inner
dimension of such a quest, and seem to mark a significant departure from social ethics. However,

the kinds of tension and conflict between self and society, featured so prominently in current psychological and philosophical literature, are not the concerns of Chung-yung. The notion that an individual's search for spiritual purity is inevitably at odds with his social responsibility is, in fact, contradictory to Chung-yung's basic assumptions.[1] This should become evident in the course of our discussion.

It is not difficult to see that the notion of the irreconcilability of self and society is frequently predicated on an unexamined proposition that the growth of one's individuality necessitates a denial of one's sociality. To be sure, the failure to develop a healthy personality can sometimes be attributed to invidious forms of social coercion. It can also be argued that the struggle for self-identity must at times involve efforts to free oneself from the dominance of outside influences. But only in an extreme display of individualism would we find a total rejection of the value of society. Indeed, even the religious recluse's renunciation of the whole world and the political anarchist's repudiation of the entire system do not question the worth of human relations such as friendship and comradeship. In the case of Chung-yung, self-cultivation itself entails not only inner conscientiousness but altruism as well. It is therefore not just undesirable but inconceivable in this view that one could ever become a profound person (an ideal personality) without being constantly in touch with people in daily human affairs. But what exactly is Chung-yung's understanding of human-relatedness?

The quest for self-cultivation in Chung-yung is never conceived as an individual's lonely struggle to achieve inner peace. In the Confucian tradition as a whole, although decisions to leave society and to dwell in the wilderness as hermits are sometimes respected as agonizing choices of great men in extremely painful situations, the deliberate attempt to segregate one's life from common human associations is always deprecated as an expression of self-centeredness. Of course, during the mourning period, one must observe the ritual of abstinence and live in relative seclusion, sometimes for as long as eighteen months. But even then, the emphasis is on the proper channeling of intense emotions and on the symbolic significance of honoring the dead, rather than on the act of self-imposed isolation. In fact, as a public institution, the central concern of the mourning ritual is not only the proper behavior of a single individual but also its influence upon social solidarity.[2] In a deeper sense, however, mourning ritual cannot be understood simply in terms of its functional role in society. We must delve into the basis of human-relatedness to find its roots.

An understanding of this key issue requires first
an examination of the concept of "filial piety"
(hsiao) in Chung-yung.

Commonly rendered as "reverence for parents,"
filial piety is considered by many to be the prime
virtue in Confucian ethics and the basis of its
understanding of proper human relations. It is
often suggested that filial piety, as a form of hierarchically defined obedience, provides the theoretical foundation for an autocratic polity.[3] Though
this may well be an accurate description of how
filial piety has actually been used in traditional
Chinese political culture, it does not follow that
it was originally intended to be so in the Confucian
tradition. Indeed, the Confucian concept of filial
piety is only marginally connected with political
control. It was not conceived as a basis for exercising autocratic power. In the case of Chung-
yung, filial piety functions primarily as an ethicoreligious symbol. Despite its nonpolitical nature,
however, the symbol does present a remarkably coherent picture, delineating how an ethical system,
centered on a particular dyadic relationship, can
become politically significant. This is not to say
that there is an explicit argument to that effect
in the language of Chung-yung, but we can reflect
upon Chung-yung's insights on filial piety with a
view to formulating an interpretation of what the

underlying structure seems to be.

It is true that, in the Confucian tradition, the father-son relationship is not only dyadic and hierarchic but also absolutely binding. Even in extraordinary circumstances, there is little justification for one to break away completely from its requirements.[4] A concern for social solidarity is certainly one of the most important reasons that this relationship is particularly emphasized. A filial son is likely to be watchful over his personal conduct, conscientious about family affairs, responsive to social obligations and, as a result, qualified for political assignments, so the argument goes. It is therefore the belief of many Confucians that filial sons often turn out to be loyal ministers. Filiality is consequently valued as an important instrument for fostering political leadership. The social function of filial piety, however, is predicated on an awareness that the father-son relationship is a primordial tie, charged with strong and persistent human emotions. Without a recognition of this affective dimension, our analysis will remain superficial.

Chung-yung characterizes the filial son in terms of his ability to "continue" (chi) the "will" (chih) and to "transmit" (shu) the "work" (shih) of his father [XIX:2]. The filial son is not necessarily an obedient son. An obedient son follows the

instructions of his father without questioning the
underlying intention of those instructions, but the
filial son must try to understand the general direction of his father's inner thoughts as well as his
expressed wishes. The filial son is therefore responsible both for what his father has actually said
and for what he has left unsaid. When filial piety
is understood as the continuation, indeed the actualization of the father's will, it involves an appreciation not only of the father's existential situation but also of his ideal self-image.

On the surface, filiality is biologically determined. Yet it is vitally important for a full understanding to realize that as a form of primordial tie,
the father-son relationship creates values of profound social significance that cannot be fully appreciated in terms of their genetic origins alone.
To be filial is not merely to continue a family line.
It is true that, following a statement in the Book
of Mencius, it has been a strong folk belief in
China that the failure to produce male progeny is
among the most serious kinds of unfilial behavior.
This may give one the impression that filial piety,
as reverence for parents, entails the primary obligation of continuing the biological line of the
family. Whether the word "posterity" (hou) in
the injunction of Mencius refers to a specific
pattern of lineal continuity, its main concern is

the ethicoreligious obligation of the son to his father.[5]

The injunction that the son "transmit the work of his father" reminds one of Confucius' assertion that he was a "transmitter" rather than a "maker."[6] Transmission, unlike making, involves a commitment to the continuous well-being of a chosen heritage. To undertake such a commitment, one must have a sophisticated appreciation of the strength and limitation of that which is to be inherited. Without such a critical awareness, "believing in and loving the ancients"[7] indicates no more than a nostalgic attachment to the past. But the Confucian choice obviously signifies that transmission is more profound and more difficult than making. For one thing, the person who transmits is indebted to the origins of his own existence. He feels a strong moral obligation toward those who significantly contributed to the formation of his own tradition. His mission, then, is not merely to adapt himself to his immediate environment but to see to it that the new world he attempts to shape is truthful to the intentions of his forefathers. Accordingly, transmission is not simply making something new but, in doing so, undertaking the responsibility of handing down the wisdom of the old as well. Thus it involves both moral obligation and historical consciousness.

It is suggestive that Chung-yung venerates King Wu and the Duke of Chou as exemplars of "extending filial piety" (ta-hsiao) [XIX:17]. According to the legend, their father, King Wen, the leader of the principality of Chou, suffered much at the hands of a debauched tyrannical ruler, the last king of the Shang dynasty (1766?-1122? B.C.). King Wen, an honorific title bestowed posthumously by his filial sons, tried to keep the tyrant in check by friendly persuasion, but failed and was put in jail.[8] During his imprisonment, he is alleged to have so significantly refined the I Ching that it has become not only a book of divination but also a book of wisdom. King Wen himself never engaged in any outright rebellion; his conciliatory attitude, according to traditional interpretations, is amply demonstrated in the "judgments" of the I Ching.[9] Yet by his moral rectitude he was able to rally the majority of the principalities around the Chou banner. Even before the commencement of the "righteous campaign" against the Shang tyrant, the direction of the Mandate of Heaven had already become apparent. Nevertheless, the actual battle that destroyed the Shang dynasty was fought by King Wu, and it was under the tutelage of the Duke of Chou that the new dynasty became fully established.[10] What the brothers accomplished, then, was the continuation of their father's will and the transmission of their father's work.

However, King Wu's "righteous campaign" against
the tyrant is said to have been launched with such
a sense of urgency that he did not even take enough
time to perform a proper burial for his father.[11]
This was certainly an overt impropriety against one
of the most sacred Confucian rites, the mourning
ritual. King Wu's irreverent attitude toward the
mourning ritual and all its symbolic associations
cannot be explained in terms of filial piety in the
context of the family. There is no provision in
the "family rituals" for such an act, no matter how
lofty the motivation may seem. The justification
has to be found beyond the normal confines of familial relationship. Comparably, it is said that
the Duke of Chou, in his determined effort to con-
solidate the dynasty, led punitive campaigns against
his own brothers.[12] The Duke's actions can hardly
be sanctioned by the rules governing the five basic
human relationships. If taken at their face value,
they can easily be interpreted as fratricidal. His
filiality must also be justified on other grounds.

An equally significant case is Chung-yung's
choice of Shun, the legendary sage-king, as the
paradigmatic example of a filial son. According to
a well-known account of Shun's predicament, he was
surrounded by a ruthless father, an iniquitous step-
mother, and a hostile half-brother.[13] To be sure,
Shun's ability to harmonize family relations under

extremely difficult conditions was a clear demonstration of his filial love. But from the perspective of Chung-yung, the outstanding manifestation
of Shun's "great filiality" (ta-hsiao) was his inner strength that enabled him to become a benevolent
ruler despite his personal plight. Indeed, he frequently had to depart from established rituals and
to suffer the accusation of being unfilial in order
to do what he believed to be right. His marriage
is a case in point. As legend has it, Shun's involvement with governmental affairs was so extensive that his simple wedding ceremony was conducted
without the prior consent of his father. This was
an obvious violation of the established decorum;
it could have seriously strained the father-son relation.[14] But in the perception of Chung-yung, the
kind of filiality Shun demonstrated, like that of
King Wu and the Duke of Chou, is predicated on a
higher morality:

> Shun was indeed greatly filial! In virtue
> he was a sage; in honor he was the Son of
> Heaven [emperor]; and in wealth he owned
> all within the four seas. Temple sacrifices
> were made to him, and his descendants pre-
> served the sacrifice to him. Thus it is
> that he who possesses great virtue will
> certainly attain to corresponding position,
> to corresponding wealth, to corresponding
> fame, and to corresponding long life. [XVII:1-2]

Filiality so conceived is certainly more than familial obligation and personal affection. To serve one's parents and make them comfortable is only to "nourish the mouth and belly" (yang k'ou-t'i).[15] Unless one can also honor one's parents in one's moral rectitude, public service, and ethical leadership, one cannot be said to have "nourished their will" (yang-chih).[16] It is in this sense that the maintenance of an ancestral line is not merely the biological prolongation of the life of a family. Rather, it signifies the continuation of a personality ideal exemplified by the forefathers of the ancestral line and the transmission of cultural values created by its outstanding members.

Mencius once remarked, "Keeping one's parents when they are alive is not worth being described as of major importance; it is treating them decently when they die that is worth such a description."[17] On the surface, Mencius may seem to have placed too much emphasis on ancestral worship, as if honoring one's parents after they have passed away is more of a virtue than serving them when they are still alive. Actually "treating them decently when they die" indicates that filiality, as an overall commitment to one's origin of existence, is a lifelong task. To serve one's parents for the duration of their lives is only a part of this overall commitment. Confucius himself stresses the same point:

"Nowadays a filial son is just a man who keeps his parents in food. But even dogs or horses are given food. If there is no feeling of reverence, wherein lies the difference?"[18] As Tseng Tzu observed in the Analects, "Let there be a careful attention to perform the funeral rites of parents, and let them be followed when long gone with the ceremonies of sacrifice; then the virtue of the people will resume its proper excellence."[19]

Tseng Tzu's statement has frequently been interpreted as a Confucian method of using rites and ceremonies to advance the virtue of the people. It is true that in the Confucian tradition rites and ceremonies are integral parts of moral education, and since the Confucian attitude toward spirits and ghosts is basically humanistic, sacrificial practices, such as those employed in ancestral worship, are often manifestations of ethical concerns. However, the interconnection between mourning rituals and sacrificial ceremonies, on the one hand, and public morality, on the other, is predicated on the existence of a sense of community, without which the following quotation from Chung-yung would not make much sense:

The ceremonies of sacrifices to Heaven and Earth are meant for the service of the Lord on High, and the ceremonies performed in the ancestral temple are meant for the service

of ancestors. If one understands the ceremonies of sacrifices to Heaven and Earth and
the meaning of the grand sacrifice and the
autumn sacrifice to the ancestors, it would
be as easy to govern a kingdom as to look
at one's palm. [XIX:6]

Underlying this seemingly simplistic causal relationship between correct ceremonies and the government of a kingdom is a set of highly complex assumptions. If we read Chung-yung with some care, we notice that the establishment and implementation of
ceremonies depend not only on sagely efforts but
also on the participation of the entire populace.
Therefore, we observe that when "Duke Chou carried
to completion the virtue of King Wen and King Wu,"
he had to ensure a communal involvement in the
ritual process:

He honored T'ai and Chi with the posthumous
title of king. He sacrificed to the past
reigning dukes of the house with imperial
rites. These rites were extended to the
feudal lords, great officers, officers, and
the common people. . . . The rule for one
year of mourning for relatives was extended
upward to include great officers, but the
rule for three years of mourning was extended upward to include the Son of Heaven.
In mourning for parents, there was no difference for the noble or the commoner. The
practice was the same. [XVIII:3]

Furthermore, in a strict sense, ceremonies cannot be artificially constructed; they must be formulated in accordance with the spiritual orientation
of the established rituals in society. When Tzu
Kung (Tz'u) proposed to do away with the sacrificial
lamb offering at the announcement of each new moon,
Confucius said, "Tz'u! You love the lamb, but I
love the rite."[20] Indeed, it was not the abolition
of a specific ceremonial act that bothered Confucius,
but the symbolic significance of ritual practices as
a whole. This by no means suggests that all ceremonial acts are so much an integral part of a complicated ritual system that any change in one of
the acts inevitably leads to a restructuring of the
whole system. It does mean, however, that despite
their formalistic nature, ceremonies are concrete
manifestations of the ethicoreligious intent underlying an established rite. Since ceremonies become
associated with a ritual system through long and complicated evolutional processes, any attempt to treat
them in isolation is likely to inflict irreparable
damage on the system itself.

In the case of ancestral worship, Chung-yung
describes the ceremonial acts of filial sons as
follows:

> In spring and autumn they repaired their
> ancestral temple, displayed their ancestral

vessels and exhibited the ancestral robes,
and presented the appropriate offerings of
the season. The ritual of the ancestral
temple is in order to place the kindred on
the left or on the right according to the
order of descent. This order in rank is
meant to distinguish the more honorable or
humbler stations. Services in the temple
are arranged in order so as to give distinction to the worthy [according to their
ability for those services]. In the
pledging rite the inferiors present their
cups to their superiors, so that people of
humble stations may have something to do.
In the concluding feast, honored places
were given people with white hair, so as to
follow the order of seniority. To occupy
places of their forefathers, to practice
their rites, to perform their music, to
reverence those whom they honored, to love
those who were dear to them, to serve the
dead as they were served while alive, and
to serve the departed as they were served
while still with us: this is the height
of filial piety. [XIX:3-5]

The historical and sociological reasons behind
the formation of these ceremonial acts may have been
forever lost, but each ritual, no matter how tri-
fling it appears to us today, seems to have symbol-
ized a sacrificial tradition with generations of
devoted observance. To sons who are filial in Chung-
yung's sense, repairing their ancestral temple, for
example, must have been a solemn occasion, observed

year after year without any conscious deviation from the prescribed methods. Similarly, the display of the ancestral vessels and the exhibition of the ancestral robes must have been performed with utmost seriousness as manifestations of their commitment to ancestral worship. The other ceremonial acts must also have been understood as significant parts of their impeccable record of filiality.

For a traditional Confucian, ancestral worship by filial sons may be taken as the microcosm of an ideal society. Ceremonial acts in this connection symbolize desirable behavioral patterns. To be sure, the overall structure is hierarchically determined, but the criteria for judging one's worth are based upon virtue and ability as well as upon age and status. To respect the old and to honor the dead is to show special concern for the common origin of all. The old are respected not only for their past service but also for the continual value of their wise guidance. The dead are honored because the loving memory of the forefathers brings forth communal identity and social solidarity. Society so conceived is not an adversary system consisting of pressure groups but a fiduciary community based on mutual trust. Only in this sense was Confucius able to make the claim that if the ruler can administer his state with rites, he will no longer have any difficulty.[21]

The thesis that governing a kingdom is no more than the political corollary of understanding proper sacrificial ceremonies may seem to us incredibly simpleminded. The reasoning behind it, however, does not depend upon a mere inference from the proposition that the primary concern of government is the correct observance of rituals. Rather, it points to a perception of politics that is significantly different from the idea that politics is basically the science or art of government. To be sure, politics is concerned with the organization, direction, and administration of all governmental units involved in the regulation and control of people in a given society. And its function is much broader than what is normally known as the ceremonial duties of the state. Yet, in the Confucian tradition, politics means "rectification" (cheng).[22]

Thus, the goal of politics is not only to attain law and order in a society but also to establish a fiduciary community through moral persuasion. The function of politics then is centered on ethical education. Of course, in our ordinary use of the term, politics can also be considered a branch of moral philosophy, dealing with the ethical relations and duties of governments. But the Confucian concept of politics as rectification involves many aspects of ethicoreligious thought that are not usually associated with the political arena.

Of primary importance is the fact that the
project of rectification is originally aimed not
so much at the people as at the ruler himself. The
idea is that the ruler, for the sake of his leadership, must engage in the rectification of his personal character. This has frequently been interpreted as a form of moral elitism, which holds that
the exemplary leadership of the ruling elite is all
that is necessary for ensuring the stability of society. Since the people are submissive, like the
grass, and the leaders are powerful, like the wind,
the influence of the ruler will surely bend the people in his direction.[23] But the original thesis only asserts the primacy of rectifying the ruler's
personal character as a precondition for good government. That the moral rectitude of the ruler necessarily brings about a good government is a deriva-
tive of the original thesis. Indeed, the original
premise is predicated on the belief that the governing process is not a control mechanism based upon
impersonal factors but a manifestation of the art
of moral persuasion. To ensure the participation
of dedicated persons at all levels of the governing
process, the quality of the ruler's personal character is of great significance.

The governmental measures of King Wen and
King Wu are spread out in the records. With

their kind of men, government will flourish.
When their kind of men are gone, their government will come to an end. When the right
principles of man operate, the growth of government is rapid, and when the right principles of soil operate, the growth of veg-
etables is rapid. Indeed, government is
comparable to a fast-growing plant. Therefore the conduct of government depends upon
the men. The right men are obtained by the
ruler's personal character. [XX:1-4]

This statement in Chung-yung directly links the
nature and function of government with the personalities of those who are actively involved in the governing process. Despite its seeming simplicity, the
statement is full of far-reaching implications. For
example, it asserts the inseparability of morality
and politics. The moral integrity of the ruler, far
from being his private affair, is thought to be a
defining characteristic of his leadership. He must
realize that what he does in private is not only
symbolically significant but has a direct bearing
on his ability to lead, for the kind of people he
can attract to take responsible positions in the
government depends, in large measure, upon his personal character. Without the participation of qualified personnel, the conduct of government, unlike
the growth of plants, will be slow and stagnant.
The ruler's moral integrity is therefore an indis-

pensable condition for good government.

If the ruler's cultivation of his personal
character is of great political significance, what
does it actually entail? <u>Chung-yung's</u> suggestion
is as follows:

> The cultivation of the person is to be ac-
> complished through the Way, and the cultiva-
> tion of the Way is to be done through human-
> ity. Humanity (<u>jen</u>) is [the distinguishing
> characteristic of] man, and the greatest ap-
> plication of it is in being affectionate to-
> ward relatives. Righteousness (<u>i</u>) is the
> principle of setting things right and proper,
> and the greatest application of it is in
> honoring the worthy. The relative degree
> of affection we ought to feel for our rela-
> tives and relative grades in the honoring
> of the worthy give rise to the rules of
> propriety (<u>li</u>). [XX:4-5]

This short passage includes three salient points in
Confucian symbolism: <u>jen</u> (humanity), <u>i</u> (righteousness), and <u>li</u> (rules of propriety). Again, <u>Chung-</u>
<u>yung</u>, in a highly condensed form, states what must
have involved a complicated structure of assumptions.
<u>Jen</u>, the cardinal concept in the <u>Analects</u>, is char-
acterized by one word: "man" (person). In Chinese
it reads "<u>jen</u> is <u>jen</u>." The first <u>jen</u> means humanity
and, since there is no gender in Chinese grammar,
the second simply refers to person. As Wing-tsit

Chan has pointed out, "it is not just a pun, but an important definition of the basic Confucian concept of humanity, for to Confucianists, the virtue of humanity is meaningless unless it is involved in actual human relationships."[24] This saying also appears in the Book of Mencius where Master Meng is alleged to have remarked, "Humanity is [the distinguishing characteristic of] man. When embodied in man's conduct, it is the Way."[25] If the Way is understood in this sense, then "the cultivation of the person" in the passage above is the process of embodying humanity in one's conduct. Does this mean that the ruler's cultivation of his personal character entails no more than the improvement of his human relationships?

Human-relatedness is certainly an integral part of self-cultivation, but one's ability to maintain continuous association with other human beings is predicated on an ever-deepening realization of one's inner morality. Mencius, despite his being fully aware of the importance of politics and language, never attempts to define human beings as political animals or symbol users. Instead, he advocates the intrinsic goodness of human nature. Implicit in this particular concern is his strong belief in the perfectibility of human nature through self-effort. Human beings are thought to be moral beings. This does not mean that in an existential sense human

beings are already good; it only asserts that the
ultimate ground of one's becoming good is located
within oneself.[26] Jen, in this sense, signifies
the fullest manifestation of humanness. A man of
humanity is thus a paradigm of the most genuine and
authentic human being, for he is able to realize
that which is common to us all. Every human being
is capable of love, but the man of humanity has already embodied love in his daily conduct.

In practice, however, a gradual process of extension is required. Since self-cultivation entails
the manifestation of one's inner morality in the context of human relationships, it seems natural that
one should take a common human feeling as one's point
of departure. The Confucian contends that one cannot
simply bypass one's primordial ties in order to demonstrate a general love for mankind.[27] If one is in-
capable of caring for one's proximity of blood, one
can hardly talk about universal love in a real experiential sense. Being "affectionate toward relatives" is therefore taken as the "greatest application" of humanity, because it indicates an immediate
extension of one's inner morality. According to this
line of thinking, whether the ruler's cultivation of
his personal character is sincere can best be judged
by his relationship to those who are closest to him.

To be sure, placing a great emphasis on one's
own relatives smacks of nepotism, or at least a form

of particularism. The thrust of the argument, however, is to go beyond any special interest group so
that the ruler can extend his leadership to embrace
the whole universe. The ruler's affection for his
relatives is thought to be only a concrete manifestation of this broad human concern. If he cannot
even show that he is affectionate toward his relatives, it is difficult for the Confucians to believe
that he can truly care for the people. On the other
hand, if his attention is only focused on his relatives, he is no more than a narrow-minded nepotist.
This is a form of particularism only in the sense
that concrete steps are to be taken in the realization of a general humanist ideal. A sense of judgment is therefore required. The concept of i, which
originally means right and proper, specifically refers to this sense of judgment, without which "concrete steps" cannot be judiciously taken. Caring
for the beloved must thus be coupled with "honoring
the worthy." Only then can the ruler provide an
impartial leadership in his government.

Explicitly defined as fitness or appropriate-
ness, i mediates between the universal principle of
humanity and the particular situations in which the
principle is concretely manifested. Furthermore,
in the words of Mencius, i is the "human path" (jen-
lu)[28] through which one's inner morality becomes
properly realized in society. What is involved here

seems to be a practical judgment based upon a holistic evaluation of objective conditions. The man
of righteousness, unlike the man of profit, is re-
solved to actualize what he believes to be just in
an equitable and open way. Accordingly, to honor
the worthy is to make sure that special respect is
accorded only to those who have made demonstrable
contributions to the state and society.

Underlying the affection of _jen_ and the justice
of _i_ is a problem of structure: by what concrete
design can relatives and those who are worthy be
affectionately and justly taken care of? A principle of differentiation is required, for to treat
the worthy as if they all belonged to the same cat-
egory or to lump all relatives together without taking into account the degrees of relatedness is simply unworkable. _Chung-yung_ suggests that it is
through considerations of this kind that the rules
of propriety become necessary.

Rendered as "ceremony," "ritual," "rites,"
"propriety," "rules of propriety," "good custom,"
"decorum," "good form," and even "natural law," _li_
signifies a structure by which _jen_ and _i_ are realized in the context of human relations. Etymologi-
cally, _li_ refers to a correct performance of sacrificial ceremonies but, as I have shown elsewhere,

the meaning of _li_ evolved from a proper act

of offering sacrifice to an authentic way of
establishing human-relatedness, which in the
Mencian version actually involves the act of
self-transformation. Li in this connection
is understood as movement instead of form.
The emphasis is on its dynamic process rather
than its static structure.[29]

It is true that the concept of li in Chung-
yung still retains a very strong sacrificial com-
ponent, but human-relatedness is so much an integral part of it that li can be conceived as a process of humanization, for he who actively partici-
pates in ceremonial acts must cultivate his human
relationships. To reiterate an earlier point, the
claim that "if the ruler can administer his state
with rites, he will no longer have any difficulty"
is predicated on the assumption that only he who
has fully harmonized his human relationships is
capable of administering his state with rites. And
since the harmonization of human relationships requires and entails a process of self-transformation,
the proper administration of the state with rites
further demands the rectification of the ruler's
personal character. Chung-yung, however, perceives
this in terms of a set of expanding concentric cir-
cles:

Therefore the ruler must not fail to culti-

vate his personal life. Wishing to cultivate his personal life, he must not fail to
serve his parents. Wishing to serve his
parents, he must not fail to know man.
Wishing to know man, he must not fail to
know Heaven. [XX:7]

As in the "eight steps" of the Great Learning,[30]
what Chung-yung intends to stress here is not a set
of causal relationships. On the surface, "wishing
to cultivate his personal life, he must not fail to
serve his parents" may seem to suggest that self-
cultivation is predicated on serving one's parents.
In the light of Chung-yung's spiritual orientation,
however, we can safely argue that the proper way of
serving one's parents is also dependent on self-
cultivation. Indeed, one becomes truly filial, according to this line of thinking, only if one's
filiality is expressed not as an obligation toward
an outside authority but as an integral part of one's
self-realization. "Wishing to cultivate his personal
life, he must not fail to serve his parents" can thus
be interpreted to mean that self-cultivation is not
only an isolated quest for inner spirituality but
also a continuous attempt to interpersonal communication. For its own completion, self-cultivation
must be extended beyond the existence of the physical self. Therefore, as a process of extension, the
cultivation of one's personal life necessarily in-

volves the effort of serving one's parents.

By analogy, filiality is not restricted to one's proximity of blood. As the cases of King Wu, Duke Chou, and Shun have indicated, to continue the will and to transmit the work of one's father requires a much broader concern for humanity. In Chung-yung's mode of thinking, however, the ultimate manifestation of self-realization transcends even the restrictions of anthropocentrism. Thus, "wishing to know man, he must not fail to know Heaven." We will return to this last point and discuss it in some detail in the next chapter.

Having discussed the relevance of the ruler's self-cultivation to political leadership, Chung-yung now turns attention to the five "universal ways" (ta-tao), three "universal virtues" (ta-te), and nine "principles" (ching) of government. The idea of politics as rectification comes through vividly in these remarks:

> There are five universal ways [in human relations], and the way by which they are practiced is three. The five are those governing the relationship between ruler and minister, between father and son, between husband and wife, between elder and younger brothers, and those in the intercourse between friends. These five are universal paths in the world. Wisdom, humanity, and courage, these three are

the universal virtues. The way by
which they are practiced is one. [XX:8]

The five "universal ways" are more often re-
ferred to in Confucian literature as either the
"five constancies" (wu-ch'ang) or the "five orders"
(wu-lun). Although they are not meant to be comprehensive, they do represent, in the eyes of the
Confucianist at least, basic human relations. Since
their claim to universality is based on commonly experienced modes of human-relatedness, they signify
no more than five ordinary manners of human interaction. Despite their commonality, however, each
of them is a world in itself. So far as interconnectedness among them is concerned, we can neither
generalize, in terms of one particular form of relationship, nor specify which among them really occupies the most prominent position.

To be sure, the father-son relationship has
been much emphasized in Chung-yung, especially in
reference to filial piety, and it is often assumed
to have been the model for the ruler-minister relationship as well. But the father-son relationship
is only one of the five basic human relations; it
would be highly contrived to have the other four
simply fall into its embracing scheme. Even in the
case of the relation between ruler and minister, the
applicability of the father-son model is still quite

limited. For example, while father and son are
bound by inseverable primordial ties, the minister
can choose to leave the ruler on grounds of incompatibility.[31] Indeed, one can decide not to serve
the state because the political milieu is damaging
to one's moral rectitude and thus refuse to enter
into any form of ruler-minister relationship.

Furthermore, the five relationships are governed by five carefully selected moral principles,
each representing an important dimension of human
community. The prominence of ethical education is
evident. In the words of Mencius, it is the rationale of how the relations actually came into existence:

> According to the way of man, if they are
> well fed, warmly clothed, and comfortably
> lodged but without education they will be-
> come almost like animals. The Sage (Em-
> peror Shun) worried about it and he appointed
> Hsieh to be minister of education and teach
> people human relations, that between father
> and son, there should be affection; between
> ruler and minister, there should be righ-
> teousness; between husband and wife, there
> should be attention to their separate func-
> tions; between old and young, there should
> be a proper order; and between friends,
> there should be faithfulness. Emperor Yao
> said, "Encourage them, lead them on, rectify
> them, straighten them, aid them, so they
> discover for themselves [their moral nature],

and in addition, stimulate them and confer kindness on them."[32]

This legendary account tells us that the humanistic concerns of sage-kings are manifested in the five moral principles of human interaction: ch'in (affection), i (righteousness), pieh (separate functions), hsü (order), and hsin (faithfulness). The concept of pieh in governing the relationship between husband and wife needs some explanation. Obviously, the emphasis is not on romantic love but on socially defined roles. Since the primary function of the husband is public service, often conducted away from home, and that of the wife is family affairs, it is important that each attend to a separate responsibility without impairing their conjugal relationship. Similarly, brothers should have a sense of orderliness in terms of seniority without losing their fraternal love, and friends should have confidence in each other.

It may not be farfetched to suggest that the five moral principles, as integral parts of Confucian ethical education, are intended to evolve a fiduciary community through five basic forms of human communication. A fiduciary community so evolved is a society of mutual trust instead of a mere aggregate of individuals. In such a soceity, the goal of the people is not only to live in peace but also to aid each other in moral exhortation for the sake of cultivating their own personal characters. It is in this sense that the three "universal virtues" are all perceived in terms of human-relatedness.

In his comments on the Analects, Wing-tsit Chan points out that

> in the Confucian ethical system, humanity and wisdom are like two wings, one supporting the other. One is substance, the other is function. The dual emphasis has been maintained throughout history, especially in Tung Chung-shu (c.179-c.104 B.C.) and in a certain sense in K'ang Yu-wei (1858-1927). Elsewhere, courage is added as the third virtue, and Mencius grouped them [humanity and wisdom] with righteousness and propriety as the Four Beginnings.[33]

Based upon a general observation of this kind, we can begin to explore what may be called the "priority of virtues" in the Confucian ethical system. To be sure, wisdom and courage are among the most often mentioned virtues in interpretive literature on Confucianism, and it seems sensible that they are grouped together with humanity to form the three universal virtues.

But while wisdom is never considered the highest manifestation of morality, and courage is included neither in the "Four Beginnings" (ssu-tuan)

nor in the "Five Virtues" (wu-te), humanity is unequivocally the cardinal symbol in Confucian humanism. Therefore, in the Confucian tradition, although
it is understandable that a wise man or a courageous
man is not necessarily a man of humanity, it is inconceivable that a man of humanity does not also em-
body wisdom and courage. This kind of priority can
be demonstrated from the fact that the classical formulations of the basic Confucian structure of vir-
tues--"the cardinal virtue," "the two primary virtues," "the three universal virtues," "the four primordial virtues (or the Four Beginnings)," and "the
five constant virtues"--can all be seen as a progres-
sive articulation of the concept of humanity (jen):

Humanity

Humanity-Wisdom

Humanity-Wisdom-Courage

Humanity-Righteousness-Propriety-Wisdom

Humanity-Righteousness-Propriety-Wisdom-Faithfulness

All the other virtues can be understood as aspects of humanity. They are internally linked to
humanity, as if to enrich its inner resourcefulness.
It is in this sense that Confucius said, "The man
of humanity is naturally at ease with humanity. The
man of wisdom cultivates humanity with facility."[34]
By analogy, courage is not only physical bravery but

also moral valor; righteousness is not only legal justice but also humane fairness; propriety is not only correctness in sacrificial ceremonies but also decorum in ethical behavior, and faithfulness is basically trustworthiness in human interaction.

The three "universal virtues" are thus focused on the realization of humanity. Since Confucius insists that "a man of humanity, wishing to establish his own character, also establishes the character of others,"[35] the method of realizing humanity is suggestively described as the "ability to understand others by what is near to ourselves."[36] That which is near at hand is therefore, in principle, realizable by each human being irrespective of his level of intelligence:

> Some are born with the knowledge [of these virtues]. Some learn it through study. Some learn it through hard work. But when the knowledge is acquired, it comes to the same thing. Some practice them naturally and easily. Some practice them with facility. Some practice them with effort and difficulty. But when the achievement is made, it comes to the same thing. [XX:9]

Having insisted upon the universal applicability of the human way, Chung-yung further claims that the human way is also the political way:

He who knows these three things [wisdom,
humanity, and courage] knows how to
cultivate his personal life. Knowing
how to cultivate his personal life, he
knows how to govern other men. And
knowing how to govern other men, he
knows how to govern the empire, its
states, and the families. [XX:11]

Again, it needs to be stressed that since politics
is understood as a process of rectification, the art
of government can be taken as an extension of moral
education. The humanization of politics, to use a
modern expression, is based on the belief that outer
kingliness requires inner sageliness. For the king-
ly way to prevail, it must follow the way of the
sages. The nine principles of government thus should
be appreciated as continuous steps toward the formation of a fiduciary community: (1) cultivating the
personal life, (2) honoring the worthy, (3) being
affectionate to relatives, (4) being respectful toward the great ministers, (5) identifying oneself
with the welfare of the whole body of officers, (6)
treating the common people as one's own children,
(7) attracting the various artisans, (8) showing
tenderness to strangers from far countries, and (9)
extending kindly and awesome influence on the feudal
lords [XX:12].

Chung-yung enumerates the benefits of pursuing

the nine principles in simple terms:

> If the ruler cultivates his personal life,
> the Way will be established. If he honors
> the worthy, he will not be perplexed. If
> he is affectionate to his relatives, there
> will be no grumbling among his uncles and
> brothers. If he respects the great minis-
> ters, he will not be deceived. If he iden-
> tifies himself with the welfare of the whole
> body of officers, then the officers will
> repay him heavily for his courtesies. If
> he treats the common people as his own
> children, then the masses will exhort one
> another [to do good]. If he attracts the
> various artisans, there will be sufficiency
> of wealth and resources in the country. If
> he shows tenderness to strangers from far
> countries, people from all quarters of the
> world will flock to him. And if he ex-
> tends kindly and awesome influence over
> the feudal lords, then the world will stand
> in awe of him. [XX:13]

Underlying the simple description, however, is a
highly integrated vision of politics that can be
analyzed at several levels. On the surface, what
is being advocated basically represents a practical
hierarchy of political functions. The ruler's at-
titudes toward the worthy, his relatives, and the
great ministers seem to show no more than a capability of applying commonsense knowledge to useful, political ends. Yet we also notice that the concept

of reciprocity is being applied to all situations under consideration. In fact, the ruler is asked to relate to others in terms of their perceptions of what he ought to do as a political leader. This insistence upon his empathetic understanding of those who, in some way, come into contact with him is reminiscent of the Confucian golden rule: "Do not do to others what you would not want others to do to you."[37]

In a deeper sense, however, the ruler cannot exercise his power directly on the people; his political influence can only be extended gradually through the mediation of appointed officers. If he fails to identify himself with the welfare of those who are responsible for the execution of his policies, his leadership will be greatly weakened. What he must do, then, is to see to it that his esteem for the worthy, his care for his proximity of blood, and his respect for the great ministers do not hamper his consideration for all officialdom--including the host of subordinate bureaucrats as well. Indeed, this process of inclusion must also involve artisans, farmers, and even strangers from far countries. The ruler's moral persuasion can be truly effective only if it is conducted in the spirit of impartiality. Once the ruler's concern is limited to special interest groups, his efficacy as a leader for the whole country becomes problematical.

Furthermore, the extension of the ruler's commonsense knowledge and ordinary, daily experience to embrace the world in a fiduciary community is not simply a process of horizontal incorporation. The movement is also vertical: the ruler's capability of extending his moral persuasion is dependent upon his ability to exert a lasting impact on the minds of the people; he must go beyond his private interests in order to reach the minds of people in all classes of society. But his transforming power can never be generated by the art of politics alone; no matter how ingenious his method of government is, unless he has a profound understanding of the human condition, his political influence cannot reach very far. Indeed, it is not enough for the ruler to provide leadership, as a chain of commands extending throughout the country. The most he can achieve by that is to ensure his hegemonic authority for a limited period of time. He can certainly evoke a sense of fear among the feudal lords by sheer force, but if he does so, his influence is confined to where he can directly exercise his political and military power. The ruler who is a real king (wang), rather than a mere hegemon (pa), must cultivate a holistic vision of politics, penetrating deeply into all levels of human-relatedness. Only then will the world stand in awe of him.

Chung-yung recommends specific measures to put the nine principles into practice. At first glance, these measures seem to suggest that the moral integrity of the ruler is all that is required for the maintenance of the kingdom. Indeed, in the perception of Chung-yung, the most secure way for the ruler to relate himself effectively to his ministers, relatives, officers, the common masses, the various artisans, strangers from far countries, and the feudal lords is by the art of moral persuasion. This does not mean, however, that the ruler, in exercising his political power, relies exclusively on the moral authority of his personality and not at all on the institutionalized authority of the bureaucracy. Moreover, although Chung-yung puts much emphasis on the self-cultivation of the ruler, it is believed that unless the inner spiritual truth of the ruler is manifested in ritual behavior observable by the people, the ruler's moral integrity will not be politically significant. And Chung-yung insists that if the ruler merely acts in accordance with the prescribed rules of propriety without being himself personally committed to them, he may become a powerful hegemon, but he will never be a true king. For the ruler to assume moral leadership as a true king, he must cultivate his inner sageliness and manifest it throughout the kingdom.[38]

Accordingly, the way that Chung-yung recommends

to cultivate the personal life of the ruler is as
follows: "To fast, to purify, and to be correct in
dress [at the time of solemn sacrifice], and not to
make any movement contrary to the rules of propriety" [XX:14]. This is reminiscent of Confucius'
instruction to his most respected disciple, Yen Hui,
that to master oneself and return to the rules of
propriety is the highest manifestation of humanity.[39] The significance of "propriety" (li) in this
connection is manifold. First, it helps the ruler
to discipline his body and mind through ritual practices. Second, it creates an atmosphere in which
any act that the ruler performs has symbolic force.
Third, it defines the role of the ruler in terms of
ethicoreligious ideas. Fourth, it ritualizes politics and provides it with a structure of meaning
that transcends power relationships. And finally,
it enables the ruler to govern without himself being
directly involved in the mechanism of control.

A recognition of the functional value of propriety in regulating social relationships, however,
only scratches the surface of Chung-yung's political
insight. It is true that another highly respected
disciple of Confucius, Yu Tzu, once remarked, "Among
the functions of propriety (li) the most valuable
is that it establishes harmony. The excellence of
the ways of ancient kings consists of this. It is
the guiding principle of all things great and

small."[40] It is important to note that the harmonizing function of propriety is valued not because
it manages to gloss over substantive conflicts but
because it can assist the ruler to establish real
harmony; as a defining characteristic of a fiduciary community, it shapes the very nature of human-
relatedness. If a society is governed by the rules
of propriety, its mode of existence will rest upon
a strong sense of mutual trust despite the presence
of apparent conflicts among its subgroups.

It is not surprising that _Chung-yung_ recommends
the following as ways of encouraging the worthy:
"Avoid slanderers, keep away seductive beauties, regard wealth lightly, and honor virtue" [XX:14].
Since the worthy (_hsien_) are persons of high moral
character with preeminent ability, it is unlikely
that they will be willing to render their service
to the government out of a sense of personal loyalty
to the ruler alone. Thus, to ensure their support,
the ruler must see to it that the ethical condition
of the court is acceptable to them. This necessitates a careful scrutiny of those who are closest
to the ruler. If the inner circle of the court is
dominated by "slanderers" and "seductive beauties,"
the ruler will easily become enmeshed in sensuous
pleasures and be fooled by misinformation. Similarly, wealth corrupts, and if the ruler puts too
much emphasis on the accumulation of wealth, either

for private consumption or for public use, his sensitivity to other vital issues of the state will
be impaired. To honor virtue, in this connection,
means that the ruler must be absolutely sincere in
promoting high moral standards in the government.
Only then will the worthy be attracted to participate in the normal functions of the state. In a
fiduciary community, it is vitally important that
"good and able" (hsien-neng) members of the society find a kindred spirit in the court, for their
moral support is essential to the survival of the
community.

If Chung-yung's measures for enlisting the support of the worthy are morally uncompromising, its
approach to regulating relationships between the ruler and his kin is conciliatory in attitude: "To
give them honorable position, to bestow on them ample emoluments, and to share their likes and dis-
likes--this is the way to encourage affection for
relatives" (XX:14). Again, such a recommendation
may give the impression that Chung-yung advocates,
or at least tolerates, nepotic practices.[41] Underlying this apparent favoritism, however, is a particular concern for the ruler's primordial ties,
both as a harmonizing force in the court and as a
political symbol for the kingdom. From the point of
view the principle of "differentiated love," it is
inconceivable that the ruler could extend his com-

passion to the people without first showing affection to his own relatives. Since those who are
closely related to the ruler are frequently most
threatening to the throne, the ruler's ability to
get along with them in a spirit of harmony is an
important indication that he can successfully deal
with some of the most difficult aspects of human
relationships. This, of course, does not mean that
the ruler is given free rein to appoint his kinsfolk
to key positions in the government. On the contrary,
although the ruler is encouraged to give honor to
and bestow emoluments on his relatives, he is not
advised to share his governmental responsibility
with them. The prerogative of exercising power of
the state is the sacred responsibility of the ruler
and his ministers.

Chung-yung recommends that the way to encourage
the chief ministers is simply "to allow them many
officers to carry out their functions." As for the
officers, it recommends that the ruler "deal with
them loyally and faithfully and give them ample emoluments." Obviously, the idea of the division of
labor is an important consideration. In fact, one of
the primary concerns of the ruler is to recruit persons of real talent to the central government so
that he can confidently delegate state authority to
them.

But the mode of exercising power in a fiduciary

community is significantly different from that of
an adversary system based upon the check and balance
of pressure groups. In Chung-yung's view, the ministers and officers are not only regulators of the
bureaucratic process but also teachers of state
ritual. The bureaucratic process is not seen as
merely an objectively designed control mechanism.
It is also thought to be an elaborate ritual act
through which the people of the kingdom all become
active participants in the community. Ideally, the
ministers and officers are the ruler's messengers
who, by moral exhortation, keep the masses informed
of his political and educational endeavors. The
government in this sense, far from being a necessary
evil, is a body of persons that constitutes the moral authority of the empire. If it fails to be responsive to the demands of the people, it can be re-
placed according to the principle of the Mandate of
Heaven.[42] Therefore, it is the ruler's obligation,
both of his own family and to the people as a whole,
that the empire be governed by "good and able" ministers and officers.

In accord with the five principles just outlined, the way Chung-yung recommends for encouraging
the common masses is as follows: "To require them
for service only at the proper time [without inter-
fering with their farm work] and to tax them lightly" [XX:14]. The whole idea of mobilizing large

groups of people for huge work projects is very alien to this line of thinking. Of course, cooperative efforts, as in the construction of irrigation systems, are deemed necessary. But the emphasis is on the fundamental activity of the people, namely, agriculture. By implication, the government is warned that interference with the livelihood of the common masses is economically unsound and morally wrong.

Chung-yung's physiocratic tendency is also reflected in its recommendation concerning the way to encourage the various artisans: "To inspect them daily and examine them monthly and to reward them according to the degree of their workmanship." The attitude here is very different from the policy of noninterference toward the farmers. Although the rationale behind the apparent "double standard" in dealing with the two different occupational groups is difficult to ascertain, it seems clear that productivity in agriculture is more highly valued than craftsmanship. However, it is misleading to suggest that the text seems to imply that since the artisans are not as important as the farmers in number and in production priority, they should be tightly controlled. What Chung-yung recommends are not measures of control but ways of expressing care. Inspections and examinations in this connection are intended to provide continuous opportunities for the artisans to upgrade their workmanship and thus obtain better compensation. Indeed, if the main focus of all of Chung-yung's other recommendations is on the virtue of considerateness, it is unlikely that it would single out the artisans for coercive treatment.[43]

Even in the case of strangers from far countries, Chung-yung recommends that the ruler "show tenderness" to them. Specifically, it suggests that the ruler "welcome them when they come and send them off when they go and commend good among them and show compassion to the incompetent" [XX:13]. On the surface, this is no more than an expression of courtesy, but implicit in the recommended way of receiving people from afar is a commitment to the Confucian ideal that "within the four seas, all men are brothers."[44] The idea that those who come from far countries are, politically speaking, "aliens" is foreign to Chung-yung's mode of thinking. The ruler is advised to treat "strangers" as guests because what he oversees, far from being a political unit, is basically an ethical communion, symbolically extending way beyond its territorial scope. As Mencius points out, the ruler's ability to attract visitors from distant regions is a good indicator of his performance as a benevolent king.[45] Indeed, if he aspires to true kingship, he must consider the well-being of every person under Heaven as his personal responsibility.[46]

Furthermore, <u>Chung-yung</u> states in its ninth principle that there are five ways for the ruler to deal with his feudal lords. By implication, if the ruler wishes to become a benevolent king, he must, in addition to all of his other obligations, "extend kindly and awesome influence over the feudal lords." In other words, having demonstrated the virtues of his personal life by honoring the worthy, being affectionate to relatives, being respectful toward the great ministers, identifying himself with the welfare of the whole body of officers, treating the common people as his own children, attracting the various artisans, and showing tenderness to strangers from far countries, the ruler, in his quest for kingship, must also try (1) to restore lines of broken succession, (2) to revive states that have been extinguished, (3) to bring order to chaotic states and to support those states that are in danger, (4) to have fixed times for their attendance at court, and (5) to present them with generous gifts while expecting little when they come.

Unlike the hegemon who attempts to maintain a structure of peace among the feudal lords by wealth and power, the true king assumes the responsibility of bringing peace to all under heaven both as a protector of human societies and as a guardian of cultural values. The relationship between the king and the feudal lords is, therefore, not definable in terms of political authority alone. The king seeks to establish a fiduciary community in which existing human societies will be encouraged to perpetuate themselves and created cultural values will be defended against ruthless destruction. Thus he must not exploit the feudal lords, but should instead make known to them that the proper ritual of paying tribute to the court does not depend upon material gifts. In fact, the feudal lords should be given enough latitude to regulate the internal affairs of their respective states; they are therefore obligated to come to the court in person only once in five years.

When there are conflicts among the feudal lords, however, the king should act both as a mediator and as a judge. It is his duty to see to it that not only is peace preserved but the principle of righteousness upheld. Moreover, the king is charged with a cultural mission defined in terms of ethico-religious values transcending the brute realities of historical change. Thus it is compassion that bids the king to assist in the revival of extinguished states and in the restoration of broken lines of succession. Although he is fully aware that these things can often be accomplished only symbolically by reenacting rituals of bygone years, he knows that the symbolism of cultural continuity is of profound significance to the meaning and function of his kingdom.

We may conclude that the ways <u>Chung-yung</u> recommends for actualizing the <u>nine</u> <u>principles</u> are based on a holistic vision of human relationships. A highly complex structure of social intercourse, one that involves the hierarchical system of feudalism, is seen as an elaboration of the dyadic relationships characteristic of common human experience. As a result, an ordinary person through his own knowledge as a member of the fiduciary community is well-prepared to understand the government, including even its <u>modus operandi</u> at the most refined levels of sophistication.

CHAPTER 4

THE MORAL METAPHYSICS

The Confucian image of man as a moral being and the Confucian idea of politics as rectification cannot be fully appreciated or understood merely at the psychosocial level. Certainly, the profound person in Chung-yung can be taken as a personality ideal; but the effort of self-cultivation as a basic concern of the profound person is aimed not only at psychological integration but also at the development of his moral life. Similarly, the goal of politics is not just to achieve a high level of social solidarity but also to lay the foundation of a fiduciary community. Indeed, Chung-yung can be characterized as approaching man and politics from a moral point of view. According to this line of thinking, a person without strong moral commitment can never become a truly exemplary teacher and exert long-lasting influence upon society; a political system without a firm ethical basis can hardly provide creative leadership for the establishment of a durable pattern of social intercourse. It would be misleading, however, to suggest that what Chung-yung advocates is simply the enormous importance of moral conformity for the stability of society. In

the Confucian tradition, moral ideas are much more
than social norms. In the case of Chung-yung, the
ultimate manifestation of morality transcends social ethics and is anchored in the unity of Heaven
and man.

Ordinarily, morality is understood as, basically, a way of preserving the community in order to
save it from destruction.[1] This "human, all too human" interpretation seems to suggest that the maintenance of a social fabric is the major function of
morality. To be sure, one may, by expansion, also
regard morality as a way of maintaining the community on a certain level of solidarity and in a certain
degree of "benevolence."[2] And, as has been shown,
Chung-yung does recognize the instrumental value of
morality as a necessary condition for political stability and as an active force for social integration.

What this interpretation fails to account for,
however, is the intrinsic meaning of morality. From
the Confucian perspective, it is not social useful-
ness that determines the worth of morality. Rather,
it is morality that circumscribes the ultimate efficacy of social values. Comparable to the Kantian
idea that "morality is not properly the doctrine how
we make ourselves happy, but how we make ourselves
worthy of happiness,"[3] the Confucian position asserts
that morality is not properly the doctrine of how we
manage to gather together, but of how we make our

gathering together worthwhile. Indeed, morality is not only a means of preserving the community, it is also the very reason why the community is worth being organized in the first place.

If morality is the foundation of all forms of social togetherness, the organization and the preservation of the human community necessitates the existence of a moral order. Although the actual existence of such an order in the world may not be "the most certain of all certainties,"[4] we can safely assume that any society, without shared moral ideas among its members, cannot survive very well or very long. But the recognition of a moral order, no matter how loosely defined, involves the acknowledgment of a more basic structure upon which morality is anchored. In the Judeo-Christian tradition, God as the ground of all reality is believed to be the ultimate basis of the moral order. It is frequently observed that Christian ethics is predicated on an assumption of human inadequacy:

> The order of human existence is too imperiled by chaos, the goodness of man too corrupted by sin, and the possibilities of man too obscured by natural handicaps, to make human order and human possibilities solid bases of the moral imperative.[5]

But Chung-yung never contemplates the possibility of an almighty creator, qualitatively different from, if not wholly other than, human reality. In fact, the lack of a creation myth is not only a prominent feature of Confucian symbolism but also a defining characteristic of Chinese cosmology.

Instead of laying claim to clear and certain knowledge of the divine as the ultimate basis of morality, Chung-yung asserts positively that the common human experience is the center upon which the moral order depends. This emphasis on the moral propensity of human nature seems, on the surface, in complete accord with J. J. Rousseau:

> The fundamental principle of all morality is that man is a being naturally good, loving justice and order; that there is not any original perversity in the human heart, and that the first movements of nature are always right.[6]

However, there is no counterpart in Chung-yung of either "social contract" or "general will." And its mode of thinking cannot be characterized as Rousseauian. Of course, Chung-yung's insistence upon the goodness of human nature, the importance of education, and the necessity of self-cultivation is certainly compatible with Rousseau's spiritual orientation, but its ethicoreligious concerns differ in a fundamental way from Rousseau's views on culture and on religion.

Furthermore, as the first chapter of Chung-yung unequivocally states, human nature itself is imparted from Heaven. Although "Heaven" in the Confucian tradition is not a personal God or an omnipotent creator, it is not devoid of transcendent reference. And it is precisely in this sense that morality in Chung-yung can be said to have a transcendent anchorage. Of course this does not imply that the transcendent anchorage of morality is absolutely inaccessible to our ordinary, daily experience. Actually, Chung-yung maintains that common human experience itself embodies the ultimate ground of morality, and thus provides the theoretical basis for actualizing the unity of Heaven and man in the lives of ordinary people. Even though only the sage, as the most genuine manifestation of humanity, can fully realize the unity, each human being is practicing it daily but without a profound awareness of its true meaning.

Therefore, what Chung-yung envisions is not merely a moral community, definable in terms of harmonized social relations. Nor is it the approximation of a moral theology, laying claim to clear and certain knowledge of the natural law. Rather, it is a form of metaphysics which advocates that the ultimate reality is perceivable and realizable in the moral life of every person because human nature is potentially a genuine manifestation of that reality.

This is predicated on the assertion that human beings, by nature, share the same reality with Heaven. They are not in any sense "created" by a higher order of being that is beyond the comprehension of human rationality. And it is precisely because their essence, so to speak, is identical with that of Heaven that they are said to have partaken their nature from Heaven. In practice, however, there is no guarantee that, with his heavenly endowed nature, each human being can effortlessly form a complete union with Heaven. Moral self-cultivation is required to actualize that ideal. Although Chung-yung never addresses itself specifically to this question, the implication seems to be that the necessity of conscious endeavor, despite the lack of any ontological gap between human nature and Heaven, is prompted by a human need to become a "cocreator."[7] This leads us to an exceedingly interesting concept that is pivotal in the closing chapters of Chung-yung: ch'eng (sincerity, truth, or reality).

Immediately following the conclusion of the section in which the nine principles of government and the necessity of applying these principles in a systematic and holistic modus operandi are discussed, Chung-yung, in a summary statement, turns its attention from "politics" to "morality." Since politics as rectification has obvious ethical implications and morality as the human way is inseparable from the governing process, the distinction we have drawn between them is mainly for conceptual expediency. It is not intended to suggest that there is a sharp contrast between the two realms of concern in Chung-yung. Yet the shift of emphasis just noted enables Chung-yung to introduce an important new concept without the appearance of an abrupt change in its trend of thought:

> If those in inferior positions do not have the confidence of their superiors, they will not be able to govern the people. There is a way to have the confidence of the superiors: If one is not trusted by his friends, he will not have the confidence of his superiors. There is a way to be trusted by one's friends: If one is not in accord with his parents, he will not be trusted by his friends. There is a way to be in accord with one's parents: If one examines himself and finds himself to be insincere, he will not be in accord with his parents. There is a way to be sincere (ch'-eng) with oneself: If one does not understand what is good, he will not be sincere with himself. [XX:17]

The word ch'eng seems adequately rendered here as "sincere." However, it should become clear in the course of our discussion that, in the context of Chung-yung, ch'eng also has connotations that go beyond those of its English counterpart. If we

cling to linguistic consistency, the English expression "sincerity" must undergo a variety of meta-
morphoses to accommodate the many-sidedness of ch'-
eng. The following quotation is a case in point:

> Sincerity is the Way of Heaven. To think
> how to be sincere is the Way of man. He
> who is sincere is one who hits upon what
> is right without effort and apprehends
> without thinking. He is naturally and
> easily in harmony with the Way. Such a
> man is a sage. He who tries to be sincere
> is one who chooses the good and holds fast
> to it. [XX:18]

Ch'eng as the Way of Heaven is certainly different
from "sincerity" as a personal quality. To say that
Heaven is sincere seems to transform the idea of an
honest person into a general description of the Way
of Heaven. But before the relationship between
Heaven and man is fully understood, it is premature
to suggest that "Heaven" has been anthropormorphized
to demonstrate a human virtue of sincerity. After
all, ch'eng here is intended to show what the Way of
Heaven is and what the Way of man ought to be.

It is probably in this sense that Wing-tsit
Chan, despite his consistency in rendering ch'eng as
sincerity in the text, makes the following observation in his introductory note on Chung-yung:

The quality that brings man and Nature
together is ch'eng, sincerity, truth or
reality. The extensive discussion of
this idea in the Classic makes it at
once psychological, metaphysical, and
religious. Sincerity is not just a
state of mind, but an active force that
is always transforming things and com-
pleting things, and drawing man and
Heaven (T'ien, Nature) together in the
same current.[8]

Although, as Chan further observes, the concept of
ch'eng is not discussed in the Analects, Chung-yung's
mode of thinking, centered on this idea, is in perfect harmony with "the more mystical aspect of the
Book of Mencius."[9]

It is suggestive that in D. C. Lau's translation of Mencius, ch'eng is rendered as "true." Thus,
in a comparable passage, it reads:

If upon looking within he finds that he has
not been true to himself, he will not please
his parents. There is a way for him to become true to himself. If he does not understand goodness he cannot be true to himself.
Hence being true is the Way of Heaven; to
reflect upon this is the Way of man. There
has never been a man totally true to himself
who fails to move others. On the other hand,
one who is not true to himself can never hope
to move others.[10]

Whether it is translated as "true" or as "sincere," ch'eng definitely points to a human reality which is not only the basis of self-knowledge but also the ground of man's identification with Heaven. This seems to imply that that which enables a person to fully realize himself and to understand Heaven is inherent in his own nature. Mencius certainly subscribes to this line of thinking:

> For a man to give full realization to his
> heart is for him to understand his own
> nature, and a man who knows his own nature
> will know Heaven. By retaining his heart
> and nurturing his nature he is serving
> Heaven. Whether he is going to die young
> or to live to a ripe old age makes no dif-
> ference to his steadfastness of purpose. It
> is through awaiting whatever is to befall
> him with a perfected character that he
> stands firm on his proper destiny.[11]

In the case of Chung-yung, the Mencian position seems quite compatible with what I have characterized in chapter 1 as the profound person's ever-deepening process toward subjectivity. Ch'eng, so conceived, is a human reality, or a principle of subjectivity, by which a person becomes "true" and "sincere" to himself; in so doing, he can also form a unity with Heaven. This is predicated on the Mencian belief:

All the ten thousand things are there in
me. There is no greater joy for me than
to find, on self-examination, that I am
true to myself. Try your best to treat
others as you would wish to be treated
yourself, and you will find that this is
the shortest way to humanity.[12]

It is vitally important to note that by assert-
ing the self-sufficiency of human nature, Mencius
does not mean to underrate the salience of moral
effort. On the contrary, the premise that "all the
ten thousand things are there in me" is intended to
provide an ontological basis for self-cultivation:
"Seek and you will get it; let go and you will lose
it."[13] Whether one can penetrate deeply into one's
own subjectivity is thus dependent upon one's personal choice, but this is not to deny that "it must
involve strenuous effort at learning and earnest
effort at practice."[14] From Chung-yung's perspective, there is no conflict between the ontological
autonomy of self-realization and the existential
necessity of self-cultivation. Indeed, it is the
human way to see to it that one's inner morality becomes actualized in concrete daily affairs. After
all, yung means "the common," and ch'eng is something to be manifested in ordinary words and ordinary deeds and its meaning is understandable to the
ordinary man.[15] Yet the profound person feels that

he must exert continuous effort to realize his inner morality, as a duty to himself as well as to Heaven:

> Study it [the way to be sincere] extensively, inquire into it accurately, think over it carefully, sift it clearly, and practice it earnestly. When there is anything not yet studied, or studied but not yet understood, do not give up. When there is any question not yet asked, or asked but its answer not yet known, do not give up. When there is anything not yet thought over, or thought over but not yet apprehended, do not give up. When there is anything not yet sifted, or sifted but not yet clear, do not give up. When there is anything not yet practiced, or practiced but not yet earnestly, do not give up. If another man succeed by one effort, I will use a hundred efforts. If another man succeed by ten efforts, I will use a thousand efforts. If one really follows this course, though stupid, he will surely become intelligent, and though weak, will surely become strong. [XX:19-21]

Underlying this powerful statement on moral effort is Chung-yung's insistence on the centrality of education. To be sure, Chung-yung contends that ch'eng necessarily leads to "enlightenment" (ming): "It is due to our nature that enlightenment results from sincerity" [XXI]. But, as the very first statement in Chung-yung suggests, although our nature is imparted from Heaven, it is our duty as human beings to cultivate the Way in order to follow our heaven-endowed nature. Similarly, despite the moral propensity of our inner nature, we must do our utmost to enlighten ourselves so that we can be truly human: "It is due to education that sincerity results from enlightenment" [XXI]. Since enlightenment as a form of self-education can eventually lead to ch'eng, and ch'eng, as an irreducible human reality, necessarily implies enlightenment, "given sincerity, there will be enlightenment, and given enlightenment, there will be sincerity" [XXI]. Nevertheless, we must not form the mistaken notion that insomuch as ch'eng inevitably entails enlightenment, education becomes somewhat superfluous.

Admittedly, Chung-yung acknowledges that although each person is endowed with inner morality, the levels of awareness are not absolutely equal among people. It can even be said that some are born with the knowledge of it, some learn it through study, and some learn it through painful work. As a result, some practice self-cultivation with natural ease, some practice it with learned facility, and some practice it with difficult effort [XX:9]. But Chung-yung insists that "when the knowledge is acquired, it comes to the same thing and when the achievement is made, it comes to the same thing"

[XXI]. Inequality among human beings in intelligence and ability notwithstanding, then, a person can always improve himself through self-effort no matter how adverse his existential situation. What really matters is therefore not the quality of one's native endowments or the nature of one's immediate surroundings, but how one can make the best use of them.

Confucius' disciple, Yen Hui, was highly praised because "Hui was a man who chose the course of the Mean (Chung-yung), and when he got hold of one thing that was good, he clasped it firmly as if wearing it on his breast and never lost it" [VIII]. Despite his plight as a poverty-stricken student, he was able to devote all his time and strength to the quest for sagehood. His courage to cultivate himself in a most unfavorable environment was characterized by Confucius as a true indication of his "love for learning" (hao-hsüeh).[16] A similar case is found in Mencius' appreciation of the sage-king Shun:

> When Shun lived in the depth of the
> mountains, he lived amongst trees and
> stones, and had as friends deer and
> pigs. The difference between him and
> the uncultivated man of the mountains
> then was slight. But when he learned
> a single good word, witnessed a single

good deed, it was like water causing a
breach in the dykes of the Yangtse or
the Yellow River. Nothing could with-
stand it.[17]

Shun's willingness to improve himself with great
earnestness evidences his utmost sincerity in self-
realization.

We have pointed out in our earlier discussion
that, from the perspective of Chung-yung, Shun's
inner strength to assume the responsibility of benevolent rule despite his personal plight is the
outstanding manifestation of his "great filiality."
But it is clear that moral exertion, too, is understood to be a defining characteristic of Shun's inner strength. If a sage-king like Shun must continuously be absolutely serious about learning and
practice, how much more "strenuous effort at learning and earnest effort at practice" is required of
everyone, whether born with the knowledge of inner
morality, to fully realize himself.

It may, in fact, be useful to suggest that
"given enlightenment, there will be sincerity" refers to "moral effort" (kung-fu), whereas "given
sincerity, there will be enlightenment" refers to
"original substance" (pen-t'i). It is inconceivable
that sincerity does not entail enlightenment, but
only through education can enlightenment lead to

sincerity. It should be noted that just as "sincerity" is only one of the several possible approximations of the character ch'eng, "enlightenment" is no more than an expedient translation of the character ming, which can also be rendered as "brilliance," "intelligence," or simply "clarity." It is important, too, to remember that "enlightenment" here refers to the Confucian concept of ming rather than the Buddhist idea of wu.

As "moral effort," enlightenment implies a process of education comparable to what the first chapter of Chung-yung characterizes as "cultivating the Way." The primary concern of this education is to make manifest the moral qualities inherent in our nature. Its aim is thus to raise the level of moral self-awareness. In so doing, it is important to note, the educational locus becomes the quest for self-knowledge. Strictly speaking this form of learning can never be imposed from outside; without the willing participation of the learner, no knowledge or experience can be transmitted. Indeed, education itself is founded upon the moral resolution of the learner who, in the last analysis, is his own teacher. Education in this connection is essentially a self-enlightening process.

On the other hand, sincerity as "original substance" is by nature self-enlightening, since it is the ontological basis upon which the moral resolution of the learner becomes both the necessary and sufficient condition for education. Indeed, since to "follow human nature is called the Way," it is inconceivable that education, as cultivating the Way, can ever depart from the inner morality of the learner. Furthermore, seeing that "human nature is imparted from Heaven" and "sincerity is the Way of Heaven," education must also assume a transcendent dimension. The quest for self-knowledge may thus be construed as corresponding to a search for an understanding of Heaven. This, in fact, is precisely what Chung-yung perceives the ideal education to be and is in perfect accord with Mencius' assertion that, if we know our own nature, we can also know Heaven.

Underlying this assertion is the premise that the human way is, in an ultimate sense, identified with the Way of Heaven because they share the same ontological reality. To be sure, Heaven is by nature sincere and human beings must learn to be sincere. Yet the reason human beings can learn to be sincere is not because of Heaven's "grace" but because our nature is originally so endowed. The reason that human beings must learn to be sincere, then, is not because of any incompleteness in their ontological reality but because their existential situations make it necessary. It is in this sense that ch'eng can be rendered as "reality." Accord-

ingly, sincerity, as the most genuine manifestation
of human virtue, is also the truth and reality of
our heavenly endowed nature. The sincere, true,
and real person is what human beings ought to be,
and only then can the deepest meaning of humanity
become fully realized:

> Only those who are absolutely sincere can
> fully develop their nature. If they can
> fully develop their nature, they can fully
> develop the nature of others. If they can
> fully develop the nature of others, they can
> then fully develop the nature of things. If
> they can fully develop the nature of things,
> they can then assist in the transforming
> and nourishing process of Heaven and Earth.
> If they can assist in the transforming and
> nourishing process of Heaven and Earth,
> they can thus form a trinity with Heaven
> and Earth. [XXII]

In light of this statement from Chung-yung, we
can see that the realization of the deepest meaning
of humanity necessitates a process moving beyond the
anthropological realm. The logic seems readily understandable. To summarize our earlier discussions:
the assertion that human nature is imparted from
Heaven suggests an ontological basis upon which the
identification of human nature with the reality of
Heaven becomes possible. Since this identification
is in essence the way of man, its actualization de-

pends upon human effort. To actualize this underlying identity, however, is not to transcend humanity but to work through it. The person who embodies
ch'eng to the utmost is also a most genuine human
being. It is in this sense that he can completely
realize his own nature. The person who realizes
his own nature to the full becomes a paradigm of
authentic humanity. What is being realized, then,
signifies not only his personal humanness but humanity as such and as a whole. And since humanity is an
integral part of the "myriad things," a complete
realization of humanity must lead to the realization
of things as well.

The development, or the unfolding, of this humanistic vision in Chung-yung seems to suggest a
simple transition from the individual person to the
human community and finally to nature. Implicit in
this ontological structure, however, is a profound
sense of oneness among human beings and a strong
belief in the organismic unity of man and nature.
It is true that human nature is imparted from heav-
en, but human beings are not merely creatures and
heaven alone does not exhaust the process of creativity. In an ultimate sense, human beings, in
order to manifest their humanity, must themselves
fully participate in the creative process of the
cosmos. To be sure, they do not create ex nihilo
(nor for that matter does Heaven), yet they are

capable of assisting the transforming and nourishing process of heaven and earth.

It is true that "only those who are absolutely
sincere" can form the ultimate trinity with heaven
and earth. And, in reality, the legendary sage-
kings alone were capable of attaining such cosmic
status. Furthermore, as Confucius clearly states
in the Analects, even Yao and Shun fell short of
conferring benefit on the people and bringing sal-
vation to all.[18] The ideal of being able to assist
in the transforming and nourishing process of heaven
and earth does seem too lofty to be actualized in
concrete human affairs. But whether the paradigm
is fully realizable in the world, the ontological
assertion that there is a possibility of human participation in the cosmic creativity is itself of
great significance. It implies that the meaning of
what is normally believed to be a personal quest for
self-realization can no longer be restricted to the
psychosocial realm; moral self-cultivation necessarily assumes an "anthropocosmic" dimension. Even
though the likelihood of one's becoming completely
identified with heaven and earth is extremely limited, one's effort to become sincere is already
cosmologically meaningful.

Indeed, Chung-yung further maintains that if
one cultivates to the utmost a particular goodness,
one can also hope to exert a transforming influence

in the universe. Although this again is predicated
on the premise that only those who have attained
the state of being absolutely sincere can transform
others, the process of becoming sincerity may be conceived as a way of restructuring the world:

> Having done this [cultivated to the utmost
> a particular goodness], they can attain to
> the possession of sincerity. As there is
> sincerity, there will be its expression.
> As it is expressed, it will become conspi-
> cuous. As it becomes conspicuous, it will
> become clear. As it becomes clear, it will
> move others. As it moves others, it changes
> them. As it changes them, it transforms
> them. [XXIII]

The sincere man's ability to transform others
is reminiscent of Confucius' observation that the
virtue of the profound person is like the wind, and
when it passes over, the grass (symbolizing and
multitude) must bend;[19] thus the profound person's
transforming influence upon the people is thought
to be irresistible. Although the statement from
Chung-yung quoted above is not incompatible with
Confucius' emphasis on the power of moral persuasion
in the Analects, it seems to signify a much more refined mode of interpretation.

The process of possessing sincerity through the
cultivation of a particular goodness as well as that

of becoming absolutely sincere can be envisioned as a process toward an ever-deepening subjectivity. In light of our discussion on the profound person, this process seems to involve a twofold movement: It makes a deep penetration, as it were, into one's own ground of existence. In so doing, it helps to bring forth a more genuine and authentic manifestation of one's humanity. Simultaneously, it extends beyond the confines of one's physical self and thus takes in others as an integral part of one's quest for self-realization. It is in this sense that the possession of ch'eng, as the embodiment of a "vector," necessarily has a directional aspect. Once the direction is determined, it cannot but reveal its course. When its course becomes clear, its brilliance radiates. As a result, the person who possesses ch'eng moves, changes, and transforms others.

It should be noted that the expression "attain to the possession of sincerity" must not be construed as a goal-oriented process with ch'eng as its intended object. In a strict sense, ch'eng is not something to be obtained. Nor can there be a movement that is external to ch'eng yet aimed at the possession of it. Chung-yung makes it clear that "sincerity is self-completion, and the Way is self-directing" [XXV:1]. It means that ch'eng is not only a state of being but also a process of becoming.

Ch'eng as a state of being signifies the ultimate reality of human nature and, as a process of becoming, the necessary way of actualizing that reality in concrete, ordinary human affairs. Therefore, ch'eng symbolizes not only what a person in an ultimate sense ought to be but also what a person in a concrete way can eventually become. Indeed, it can be further suggested that in Chung-yung not only human beings but things (wu) in general are also thought to be enactments of ch'eng. And since the cosmos is conceived as the effortless self-unfolding of ch'eng, nothing can come into existence without it. Thus, "sincerity is the beginning and end of things. Without sincerity there would be nothing" [XXV:1].

Earlier it was pointed out that because of the ontological unity of human beings and the myriad things, a complete realization of humanity must lead to the realization of things as well. The self-completion of ch'eng is, therefore, not confined to the individual, nor is it restricted to the anthropological realm. Ch'eng is a self-determined process of completion; its power is self-generated, and its course of action directed from within. Yet the self-sufficiency of ch'eng makes it necessary to transcend a limited and limiting structure of expression. Thus Chung-yung asserts that "sincerity is not only the completion of one's own self, it is that by which all things are completed" [XXV:3]. It further states that

> the completion of the self means humanity.
> The completion of all things means wisdom.
> These are the character of nature,[20] and
> they are the Way in which the internal and
> external are united. Therefore whenever
> it is employed, everything done is right.
> [XXV:3]

Since ch'eng as the ultimate human reality necessarily involves ming (enlightenment), humanity must lead to wisdom. The inseparability of wisdom and humanity thus defines "the character of nature." And it is in this sense that the internal process toward subjectivity (the sincere, true, and real humanity) and the external movement toward objectivity (things in general) are united. This enables Chung-yung to conclude that, if the principle of ch'eng is appropriated in a timely way, everything done will be fitting.

It would be misleading, however, to interpret ch'eng purely in terms of the self-realization of human beings. Of course in Chung-yung's mode of thinking, it is inconceivable that ch'eng could have an ontological status beyond the comprehension of human rationality. It is therefore not entirely correct to regard ch'eng as the functional equivalent of God in Confucian symbolism.[21] But, even though Chung-yung's language does not characterize ch'eng as a creator, it can be conceived as a form of creativity:

> Therefore absolute sincerity is ceaseless. Being ceaseless, it is lasting. Being lasting, it is evident. Being evident, it is infinite. Being infinite, it is extensive and deep. Being extensive and deep, it is high and brilliant. It is because it is extensive and deep that it contains all things. It is because it is high and brilliant that it overshadows all things. It is because it is infinite and lasting that it can complete all things. In being extensive and deep, it is a counterpart of Earth. In being high and brilliant, it is the counterpart of Heaven. In being infinite and lasting, it is unlimited. Such being its nature, it becomes prominent without any display, produces changes without motion, and accomplishes its ends without action. [XXVI:1-6]

In a deeper sense, ch'eng is not merely an ordinary form of creativity; it is that which brings about the transforming and nourishing processes of heaven and earth. As creativity, ch'eng is "ceaseless" (pu-hsi), and because of its ceaselessness it does not create in a single act beyond the spatio-temporal sequence. Rather, it creates in a conti-

nuous and unending process in time and space. It
is therefore a "lasting" (chiu) event. In fact,
as it always manifests itself in concrete human
affairs, it is necessarily "evident" (cheng). However, the manifestation of ch'eng is evident not
merely because it can be objectively verified, but
also because it is a principle of subjectivity. As
an experienced reality in both of these senses, the
working of ch'eng is "infinite and lasting" (yu-chiu)
in time, "extensive and deep" (po-hou) in breadth,
and "high and brilliant" (kao-ming) in profundity.
Therefore, like earth it "contains all things" (tsai-
wu), like heaven it "overshadows all things" (fu-wu),
and since its creativity is infinite, it "completes
all things" (ch'eng-wu). Ch'eng so conceived matches
heaven and earth in its unlimited creativity, and
thus "becomes prominent without any display, produces changes without motion, and accomplishes its
ends without action."

Truly, in the language of Chung-yung, ch'eng is
reality in its all-embracing fullness. It can perhaps be characterized as the self-manifestation of
being in a multidimensional structure of existence.
Yet ch'eng is not only being but also activity; it
is simultaneously a self-subsistent and self-fulfill-
ing process of creation that produces life unceasing-
ly. "Absolute sincerity is ceaseless" specifically
points to this activity of "ever producing without

rest" (sheng-sheng pu-hsi). Ch'eng is therefore
reality in its primordial state of genuineness, the
living experience of the immediate inner self-reve-
lation of true nature, and the ultimate basis upon
which the unity of man and heaven becomes possible.
It is in this sense that Chung-yung asserts that
"the Way of Heaven and Earth may be completely described in one sentence: They are without any
doubleness and so they produce things in an unfathomable way" [XXVI:7]. And the Way of heaven and
earth can be "extensive, deep, high, brilliant, infinite, and lasting" [XXVI:8], because of its creative nature. Likewise, the "purity" (shun) of the
sage is also "unceasing." The reason the sage can
form a trinity with heaven and earth, then is because he follows the Way by realizing that which is
inherently in him.

In an exceedingly interesting passage, Chung-
yung observes the fecundity of the cosmos in extremely simple terms:

The heaven now before us is only this
bright, shining mass; but when viewed
in its unlimited extent, the sun, moon,
stars, and constellations are suspended
in it and all things are covered by it.
The earth before us is but a handful of
soil; but in its breadth and depth, it
sustains mountains like Hua and Yüeh without feeling their weight, contains the

rivers and seas without letting them leak
away, and sustains all things. The mountain
before us is only a fistful of straw; but
in all the vastness of its size, grass and
trees grow upon it, birds and beasts dwell
on it, and stores of precious things
[minerals] are discovered in it. The water
before us is but a spoonful of liquid, but
in all its unfathomable depth, the monsters,
dragons, fishes, and turtles are produced
in them, and wealth becomes abundant because of it. [XXVI:9]

This magnificent display of fecundity in heaven,
earth, mountains, and oceans does not, however, suggest the existence of an omnipotent creator. On
the contrary, it indicates the complete fruition of
that which is naturally so. Therefore, "what makes
Heaven to be Heaven" is precisely this: "Ah! profound without end (wu-mu pu-i)" [XXVI:10]. There is
no need to find an external cause as an explanation;
nor is there any urge to prove that a transcendent
and unknowable agent is really behind the scene.

Similarly, the creativity of the sage radiates,
as it were, from the inmost core of human nature.
Like the Way of Heaven and Earth, human creativeness
also manifests itself by focusing on that which is
near at hand. Just as "a handful of soil" or "a
spoonful of liquid" is the basis of the depth and
fecundity of the cosmos, so the common experience

of ordinary people serves as the foundation for the
creative transformations of the sage. In the words
of Mencius, "the sage and I are the same in kind,"
and "the sage is the first to possess what is common
in our minds."[22] By realizing humanity in its all-
encompassing wholeness, the sage transforms others
as well as himself because he also is without any
doubleness. The Way of the sage therefore is centered on the commonality of human nature. And it
is this sameness inherent in each human being that
enables the sage to establish others and to enlarge
others as a way of establishing and enlarging himself.[23] Only in this sense can the self-realization
of a single individual broaden and deepen the meaning
of humanity as a whole:

> Great is the Way of the sage! Overflowing,
> it produces and nourishes all things and
> rises up to the height of heaven. How ex-
> ceedingly great! [It embraces] the three
> hundred rules of ceremonies and the three
> thousand rules of conduct. It waits for
> the proper man before it can be put into
> practice. [XXVII:1-4]

Actually, the Way of the sage does not merely
"rise up to the height of heaven." Since the ch'-
eng of the sage is the same as the ch'eng of Heav-
en, they can be fully united. After all, as has
already been noted, the ontological reality of man

is none other than the ontological reality of Heaven. The relationship between Heaven and man is not an antinomic bi-unity but an indivisibly single oneness. In this sense, the sage as the most authentic manifestation of humanity does not coexist with Heaven; he forms a coincidence with Heaven. Accordingly, ch'eng as the ultimate reality is conceived not as the unity of opposites but as a continuous, lasting, and homogeneous whole. Despite the possibility of a conceptual separation between Heaven and man, inwardly, in their deepest reality, they form an unbreakable organismic continuum. Thus the most profound metaphysical insight begins with the common moral sense of each human being. The process toward an ever-deepening subjectivity, being the path leading into the depths of reality, is thus also the way of "transcendental thought." Indeed, as Chung-yung asserts, "unless there is ultimate virtue, the ultimate Way cannot be crystallized" [XXVII:5].

Nevertheless, it is absolutely essential to note that the ontological inseparability of Heaven and man that enables the sage to act as the co-creator of the cosmos also rules out any form of "hubris." Intent on becoming a sage, the profound person

honors the moral nature and follows the
path of inquiry and study. He achieves
the breadth and greatness and pursues
the refined and subtle to the limit.
He seeks to reach the greatest height
and brilliancy and follows the path of
Centrality and Commonality. He goes over
the old so as to find out what is new.
He is earnest and deep and highly respects
all propriety. [XXVII:6]

It is probably in this connection that Confucius
contends that "although a man occupies the throne,
if he has not the corresponding virtue, he may not
dare to institute systems of rituals and music. Although a man has the virtue, if he does not occupy
the throne, he may not dare to institute systems of
rituals and music either" [XXVIII:4]. And Confucius
himself, as an exemplary teacher of his own vision,
is said to have talked about the rituals of the Hsia
dynasty (2183-1752 B.C.?), studied the rituals of the
Shang dynasty (1751-1112 B.C.), and, having realized
the full import of them, followed the rituals of the
(Western) Chou dynasty (1111-770 B.C.).[24]

Thus, Chung-yung further maintains that true
leadership must entail a moral awareness of the existing cultural mode. Specifically, leadership involves a profound knowledge and a timely application
of the rituals, institutions, and language that
govern the fiduciary community of which the leader

is a part. Without such knowledge and application, Chung-yung argues, people would not be persuaded to participate. As a result, the community would not be a shared experience but an abstract name. The only method for the leader to develop the "Way," the "model," and the "pattern" of the world, then, is to deny hubris so that genuine humanity can be fully manifested.[25]

> Therefore the Way of the true leader is rooted in his own personal life and has its evidence among the common people. It is tested by the experience of the Three Kings and found without error, applied before Heaven and Earth and found not to be in contradiction with their operation, laid before spiritual beings without question or fear, and can wait for a hundred generations for a sage [to confirm it] without giving rise to any doubt. [XXIX:3]

Chung-yung further concludes that "there has never been a leader who did not answer this description and yet could obtain early renown throughout the world" [XXIX:6]. As a matter of historical record, who, in fact, could answer this description? Although Chung-yung never addresses itself directly to this particular question, it is not difficult to infer from passages that bear on it indirectly that only the sage-kings such as Yao and Shun and the

founding fathers of the Chou dynasty such as King
Wen and King Wu are fitting examples of the true
leader.

The uniqueness of Confucius, who was honored
by Mencius as "the one who gathered together all
that was good" (chi ta-ch'eng),[26] lies precisely
in his creative continuation of the Way of the true
leader:

> Chung-ni [Confucius] transmitted the ancient
> traditions of Yao and Shun, and he modeled
> after and made brilliant the systems of King
> Wen and King Wu. He conformed with the
> natural order governing the revolution of
> the seasons in heaven above, and followed
> the principles governing land and water
> below. [XXX:1]

His harmonizing influence gives shape and meaning
to the ancient traditions of Yao and Shun and the
ritual systems of Wen and Wu; in him, the ways of
the former kings converge into an all-embracing
unity. Furthermore, by allying himself with the
depth and fecundity of nature, he transforms the
multiple structure of seasons, land, and water into an interpenetrating whole. In doing so, he has
assisted, like the sage-kings, in the nourishing
process of heaven and earth. And thus "he may be
compared to earth in its supporting and containing

all things, and to heaven in its overshadowing and embracing all things. He may be compared to the four seasons in their succession, and to the sun and moon in their alternate shining" [XXX:2].

Just as the greatness of heaven and earth lies in the fact that "all things are produced and developed without injuring one another" [XXX:3], and that "the courses of the seasons, the sun, and moon are pursued without conflict" [XXX:3], so the uniqueness of Confucius lies in his capaciousness in allowing "the lesser virtues [to] flow continuously like river currents, and the great virtues [to] go silently and deeply in their mighty transformations" [XXX:3].

This godlike creativity of Confucius must not be conceived as the demonstration of some superhuman quality inherent in his nature. Far from being superhuman, what Confucius was able to manifest can be characterized as a "refinement" of his humanity. As Mencius aptly puts it, "the desirable is called 'good.' To have it in oneself is called 'true.' To possess it fully in oneself is called 'beautiful,' but to shine forth with this full possession is called 'great.' To be great and be transformed by greatness is called 'sage'; to be sage and to transcend the understanding is called 'divine.'[27] Thus, the "divinity," or spirituality, of Confucius is deeply rooted in his humanness. Indeed, the refined human qualities are the defining characteristics of his spirituality. Understandably,

> only the perfect sage in the world has
> quickness of apprehension, intelligence,
> insight, and wisdom, which enable him to
> be overshadowing; magnanimity, generosity,
> benignity, and tenderness, which enable
> him to be embracing; vigor, strength,
> firmness, and resolution, which enable
> him to be steadfast; orderliness, serious-
> ness, centrality, and correctness, which
> enable him to be reverent; pattern, order,
> thoroughness, and penetration, which enable
> him to be discriminative. [XXXI:1]

When these moral qualities are completely refined, they come forth in an all-pervading fullness
like the unceasing spring that overflows at all
times. Chung-yung observes that this is why "[Con-
fucius] appears and all people respect him, speaks
and all people believe him, acts and all people are
pleased with him" [XXXI:3]. But it should be re-
iterated that the appearance, speech, and action of
Confucius are thought to be confirmable by common,
everyday experience. Indeed, the ultimate authority
of Confucius is not delegated from an external source
but generated from the inner depths of his personality. He is respected and trusted not because he
is unworldly but because he is absolutely sincere

with himself. Therefore, it is on account of his humanity that

> his fame spreads overflowingly over the
> Middle Kingdom, and extends to barbarous
> tribes. Wherever ships and carriages
> reach, wherever the labor of man pene-
> trates, wherever the heavens overshadow
> and the earth sustains, wherever the sun
> and moon shine, and wherever frosts and
> dew fall, all who have blood and breath
> honor and love him. [XXXI:4]

It is only in this sense that Confucius is considered a "counterpart of Heaven" (p'ei-t'ien). Of course, "counterpart" here does not mean to suggest that Confucius is, in a sense, being deified. Whether or not Confucius has, in fact, been worshipped as a deity, what Chung-yung intends to bring out in this particular connection is simply the observation that by refining his moral qualities, Confucius has deepened and broadened the meaning of humanity to the extent that it is no longer confined to the anthropological realm.

Confucius' efficacy and potency in reaching the "virtue of Heaven" (t'ien-te) may seem to imply a form of hubris. To be sure, it is said that without depending on any external power he can "order and adjust the great relations of mankind, establish the great foundations of humanity, and know the

transforming and nourishing operations of heaven
and earth" [XXXII:1]. And the glowing comments on
his sageliness and wisdom further give the impression that Confucius is, after all, glorified as a
miraculous being:

> How earnest and sincere--he is humanity!
> How deep and unfathomable--he is ocean!
> How vast and great--he is heaven! [XXXII:2]

If we examine this mode of articulation closely,
however, it becomes clear that Chung-yung's poetic
expression, which is in the style of the Book of
Odes, simply praises the genuineness, depth, and
breadth of Confucius as a transmitter and as an
exemplary teacher.

This interpretation can be supported by the
last chapter of Chung-yung, in which several quota-
tions from the Book of Odes are cited to illustrate
the profound person:

> The Book of Odes says, "Over her brocaded
> robe, she wore a plain and simple dress,"
> for she disliked the loudness of its color
> and pattern. Thus the way of the profound
> person is hidden but becomes more prominent
> every day, whereas the way of the small
> person is conspicuous but gradually dis-
> appears. It is characteristic of the pro-
> found person to be plain, and yet people do

not get tired of him. He is simple and
yet rich in cultural adornment. He is
amiable and yet systematically methodical.
He knows what is distant with what is
near. He knows where the winds (moral
influence) come from. And he knows the
subtle will be manifested. Such a man
can enter into virtue. [XXXIII:1]

Confucius' self-image as a true learner seems
to answer this description very well. The way of
the profound person strongly suggests a sense of
humility. Only if one can "enter into virtue" (ju-
te) is there any possibility of eventually reaching
the "virtue of Heaven." That the sage can form a
coincidence with Heaven, therefore, is rooted in
his humble realization that however long the voyage,
it must begin with what is near at hand [XV:1]. The
profound person is plain, simple, and amiable, for
he knows that the ultimate manifestation of his true
nature can never be attained by breaking away from
human commonality. Thus, in a quiet and modest manner he goes about the great task of self-realization.
He does not assume an air of superiority; nor does
he pretend to have privileged access to an extraordinary truth. It is impossible to insert any
wedge, so to speak, into the continuity of his self-
realizing experience and thus create a chasm that

requires, for example, a leap of faith to bridge
it.

Yet the profound person obviously does not lead
an ordinary, unreflective existence. Although it
is not easily discernible in terms of social relations, he is a person of unusual strength. And
since his strength lies in his commitment to "learning for himself" (wei-chi chih-hsüeh),[28] he exerts
special effort at self-improvement precisely in
those areas that are beyond the scrutiny of the
public:

> The Book of Odes says, "Although the fish
> may dive and lie at the bottom, it is
> still quite clearly seen." Therefore the
> profound person examines his own heart and
> sees that there is no compunction, and
> that he is not violating his resolution.
> The profound person is unequaled in the
> fact that he [is cautious] in those things
> which people do not see. [XXXIII:2]

The strength of the profound person is, therefore,
a form of inner strength, which results from intellectual integrity and moral rectitude rather than
from a conscious attempt to gain social approval.
But despite the internality of the profound person's
quest for self-realization, its ability to produce
a persuasive effect upon others is very great:

The <u>Book of Odes</u> says, "Though the ceiling
looks down upon you, be free from shame
even in the recesses of your own house."
Therefore the profound person is reverent
without any movement and truthful without
any words. The <u>Book of Odes</u> says, "Throughout the sacrifice not a word is spoken,
and yet [the worshipers are influenced and
transformed] without the slightest contention." Therefore the profound person does
not resort to rewards and the people are
encouraged to virtue. He does not resort
to anger and the people are awed. [XXXIII:
3-4]

Thus, as a true leader of humanity, the profound
person can set in motion a process of moral transformation in society by his exemplary living without imposing any coercive measures upon the people.
Understandably, the profound person is instrumental
in the formation of a fiduciary community. His
magnetic power gathers people together for no other
external purpose than the actualization of their
own nature. Since the complete fulfillment of the
nature of human beings necessarily leads to a full
development of the nature of things, the profound
person's seemingly private quest for inner truth
entails the restructuring of sociopolitical affairs
and natural phenomena. Consequently, the profound
person's "learning for himself," a moral endeavor
to be sure, enables him to create a realm of value

that is, in a fundamental way, laden with metaphysical significance:

> The Book of Odes says, "He does not display
> his virtue, and yet all the princes follow
> him." Therefore when the profound person
> is sincere and reverent, the world will be
> in order and at peace. The Book of Odes
> says, "I cherish your brilliant virtue,
> which makes no great display in sound or
> appearance." Confucius said, "In influ-
> encing people, the use of sound and appear-
> ance is of secondary importance." The Book
> of Odes says, "His virtue is as light as
> hair." Still, a hair is comparable. "The
> operations of Heaven have neither sound
> nor smell." [XXXIII:5-6]

Thus in full circle, Chung-yung comes around
to the insight of the first chapter: "There is
nothing more visible than what is hidden and nothing more manifest than what is subtle." The profound
person, through a long and unceasing process of
delving into his own ground of existence, discovers
his true subjectivity not as an isolated selfhood
but as a great source of creative transformation.
As the inner sincerity of the profound person springs
forth an unflagging supply of moral and spiritual
nourishment for the people around him, the Confucian
ideal of society (the fiduciary community) gradually
comes into being. The continuous well-being of such

a society depends upon the cultivation of the profound person in an ever-broadening net of human relations, for self-realization in Chung-yung's view
necessarily involves a process of fulfilling the
nature of others. Thus, the great foundation and
the universal path of the world are both centered
on the transforming influence of the profound person.
The hidden and subtle way by which the brilliant
virtue of the profound person radiates outward is
colorless and shapeless, but, like the fecundity of
heaven and earth, its creative power is visible and
manifest everywhere. Yet, as Chung-yung strongly
maintains, reality in its all-embracing fullness
authenticates the concrete manifestation of common
human existence as well as the most mysterious function of the universe. And it is through self-knowledge derived from ordinary experience that the most
profound wisdom enfolds.

Notes to Preface

1. The Five Classics are the Book of Changes, the Book of Poetry, the Book of History, the Book of Rites, and the Spring and Autumn Annals. Chung-yung was originally Chapter 31 of the Book of Rites.

2. It should be noted that although Chung-yung had been treated as an independent treatise ever since the Han dynasty (207 B.C.-200 A.D.), it became widely known as a great statement on human nature in late imperial China. Li Ao (772-841), in his essays on "Returning to Human Nature," interpreted Chung-yung in the light of Mencius' philosophy. Others who were fascinated by Chung-yung included the Sung statesman Fan Chung-yen (989-1052) and the Sung philosopher Chang Tsai (1020-1077). Since the thirteenth century, a great many well-known Confucian scholars have done exegeses of the work. For Li's essays, Li Ao, Li Wen-kung chi in 18 chüan (1487 blockprint edition), 2:5a-13b. For a brief discussion on Li's thought in English, see Carsun Chang, The Development of Neo-Confucian Thought (New York: Bookman Associates, 1957), p. 106.

3. The Four Books are the Analects, the Book of Mencius, Chung-yung, and the Great Learning, another chapter in the Book of Rites. Although Chu Hsi was instrumental in the selection of the Four Books, The importance of Chung-yung as a basic Confucian classic had been recognized long before Chu Hsi's formal attempt to group them together.

4. For example, the philosophy of Mou Tsung-san, a leading Confucian thinker in contemporary China, is reflective of Chung-yung's mode of thinking. See his Hsin-t'i yü hsing-t'i (Taipei: Cheng-chung Book Co., 1968), 1:1-224. For comparable

cases, see T'ang Chün-i, <u>Chung-kuo che-hsüeh yuan-lun: yuan-hsing p'ien</u> (Hong Kong: New Asia Research Institute, 1968), pp. 1-68; Fung Yu-lan, <u>The Spirit of Chinese Philosophy</u>, trans. by E. R. Hughes (London: Kegan Paul, Trench, Trübner & Co., 1947), <u>passim</u>; and Hsiung Shih-li, <u>Tu-ching shih-yao</u> (reprint, Taipei: Kuang-wen Book Co., 1960) 1:15-17. I would also like to mention Yun Sung-bum's recent attempt to build an indigenous Korean theology on the concept of <u>ch'eng</u> (sincerity). As a leading theologian in Korea, Yun's creative appropriation of this key concept from <u>Chung-yung</u> has already been hailed as a fruitful development in theological thinking. See Yun Sung-bum, <u>Han-guk-chŏk Sinhak-sŏng ŭi Hae-sŏk-hak</u> (Seoul: Sŏn Myŏng Munwha-sa, 1972). A review of Yun's book in English by Pyun Sun-hwan is found in <u>Korea Journal</u> (February 1973). I am indebted to Mr. Young Chan Ro of University of California at Santa Barbara for this information.

5. I am indebted to Paul Ricoeur for helping me to articulate this methodological point. His lecture on "Structuralism and Hermeneutics" delivered at UC, Berkeley, on November 6, 1975 and subsequent discussions made me conscious of what I had been doing in a more critical light.

6. Especially in terms of the Mencian line of Confucianism.

7. See Roger Poole, <u>Towards Deep Subjectivity</u> (New York: Harper Torchbooks, 1972), pp. 12-43.

8. See Michael Polanyi, <u>Personal Knowledge: Towards a Post-Critical Philosophy</u> (New York: Harper Torchbooks, 1964), pp. 203-245.

9. The term "moral metaphysics" is based on Mou Tsung-san's idea of "<u>tao-te ti hsing-shang hsüeh</u>" in <u>Hsin-t'i yü hsing-t'i</u>, 1:138-189.

Notes to Chapter 1

1. Wing-tsit Chan, A Source Book of Chinese
Philosophy (Princeton, N.J.: Princeton University
Press, 1973), p. 96. It is interesting to note
that H. G. Creel observes: "Just as the Zen Buddhist claimed that their doctrine was an esoteric
teaching of the Buddha, not imparted to the common
herd, so certain Neo-Confucians maintained that the
Doctrine of the Mean embodied the esoteric teaching
of Confucius." See his Chinese Thought from Confucius to Mao Tse-tung (New York: A Mentor Book,
1960), p. 167. Although it is difficult for me to
subscribe to Creel's suggestion that Chung-yung is
"esoteric," I fully recognize that some of its discussion on the unity of man and Heaven are "mystical" in character.

2. The word chih, in this connection, also
conveys the meaning of "fully developed."

3. Although for stylistic reasons I have
occasionally departed from standard translations
of technical terms, the English version used in my
study is mainly based on Wing-tsit Chan's A Source
Book of Chinese Philosophy (Princeton: Princeton
University Press, 1973), pp. 98-113. However, for
the purpose of identification, both chapter and
section numbers are included. The division of sections is based on James Legge, trans., The Doctrine
of the Mean, in The Chinese Classics, vols. 1-2
(reprint; Taipei: Wen-hsing Book Co., 1966), pp.
382-434. Thus "I:1-5" means chapter I, sections
1 to 5.

4. For a systematic inquiry into the relationship between "centrality" and "harmony" in Confucian philosophy, see Wang Yü, Ju-chia te chung-ho
kuan (Hong Kong: Lung-meng Book Co., 1967), pp.

1-108.

5. <u>Analects</u>, XV:28. For a brief but informative discussion on the humanism of Confucius, see Wing-tsit Chan, pp. 14-18. For a general discussion on the philosophical implication of <u>Chung-yung's</u> human way, see Liu Shu-hsien, "The Confucian Approach to the Problem of Transcendence and Immanence," <u>Philosophy East and West</u> 22 (January 1972): 45-52. Also see Liu's article on "The Religious Import of Confucian Philosophy: Its Traditional Outlook and Contemporary Significance," <u>Philosophy East and West</u> 21 (April 1971):157-175.

6. See Mircea Eliade, <u>Traité d'histoire des religions</u> (Paris, 1949), p. 385. The expression of "anthropocosmic experience" is quoted in Paul Ricoeur, <u>The Symbolism of Evil</u>, trans. from the French by Emerson Buchanan (Boston, Mass.: Beacon Press, 1970), p. 11.

7. This concept of "a leap of faith" may appear to be idiosyncratically Kierkegaardian, but what I have in mind is, I believe, a widely shared concern in Christian theology. As John E. Smith has pointed out, the central problem is this: "What is the relation of religion, so conceived, to the content and form of morality? Or the question may be made more concrete by asking: What is the relation between moral standards and moral passion and that faith in God as the ground and goal of life which is the answer to the basically religious question of man's ultimate destiny?" It should become clear in the course of our discussion that the mode of questioning itself is alien to <u>Chung-yung's</u> ethicoreligious orientation. See John E. Smith, <u>Reason and God: Encounters of Philosophy with Religion</u> (New Haven, Conn.: Yale University Press, 1961), p. 196.

8. I have particularly in mind the works of

modern theologians such as Paul Tillich. For
example, see his What Is Religion, trans. by
James Luther Adams (New York: Harper & Row,
1973), pp. 72-88. In this, as well as in many
other of his seminal studies on Christianity,
Tillich claims that the divine and the secular
alike stand over against the demonic. Sin so
conceived is not an active force of evil but an
"estrangement" from God. Theologians of different persuasions may all subscribe to this
general thesis, both Harvey Cox and Thomas Merton
argue along the same line in this connection.
However, this in no way minimizes the fundamental difference betweeen Chung-yung's mode of
thinking and Christian thought.

9. Wing-tsit Chan asserts that Confucian
humanism is "not the humanism that denies or
slights a Supreme Power, but one that professes
the unity of man and Heaven"; see Chan, p. 3.
Among modern Western interpreters of Confucianism,
E. R. Hughes and D. Howard Smith are particularly
perceptive in analyzing its religious dimension.
See E. R. Hughes, trans., The Great Learning and
the Mean-in-Action (London: J. M. Dent & Sons,
1942), p. 114; and D. Howard Smith, Chinese Re-
ligions (New York: Holt, Rinehart and Winston,
1968), p. 35. Also see Huston Smith, The Re-
ligions of Man (New York: Harper & Row, 1965),
pp. 160-196, and Wilfred Cantwell Smith, The
Meaning and End of Religion (New York: Mentor
Books, 1964), pp. 64-67.

10. The term "fidelity" is taken from the
Neo-Socratic, Gabriel Marcel. See his Creative
Fidelity, trans. by Robert Rosthal (New York:
The Noonday Press, 1969), pp. 147-183. It
should be noted that while Marcel tries to elu-
cidate the relationship between man and God in

Christian symbolism, my intention here is to stress the mutuality of the human way and the Way of Heaven in the Confucian tradition. I would contend that the notion of "immediacy" is more applicable to Chung-yung's idea of sincerity (ch'eng) than to the Christian concept of faith.

11. Chung-yung's perception of humanity is significantly different from the Greek concept of man. Chung-yung does not provide us an aesthetic exclamation that "wonders are many, and none is more wonderful than man" as in the Antigone of Sophocles. Nor does it make the assertion that "man is the measure of all things" as in the Cratylus, Theatetus and Laws of Plato and the Metaphysics of Aristotle. It should become clear in the course of our discussion that Chung-yung's humanism does not resemble any form of anthropocentrism. For a comparative study of the concept of man in classical Confucianism and in Greek philosophy, see Donald J. Munro, The Concept of Man in Early China (Stanford, Ca.: Stanford University Press, 1969), pp. 49-83.

12. For a systematic presentation of Ch'ü Hsi's "method of reading" (tu-shu fa), see Ch'ien Mu, Chu Tzu hsin hsüeh-an, 5 vols. (Taipei: San-min Book Co., 1971), 3:613-687. See also Chang Tsai's remark that each sentence in Chung-yung should be experientially understood, in Chu Hsi and Lü Tsu-ch'ien, comp., Chin-ssu lu (Ssu-pu pei-yao edition), 3:15.

13. For a critical analysis of the text of Chung-yung, see Akatsuka Kiyoshi, ed., Daigaku Chūyō, in the series Shinyaku kambun taikei (Tokyo: Meiji sho-in, 1967), pp. 147-198. An examination of Akatsuka's interpretive position is found in Yamashita Ryūji, ed., Zenyaku kambun

148

taikei (Tokyo: Shūei sha, 1975), 13:177-198. For
a brief account of the problems of dating and authorship of Chung-yung, see Ts'ai Ai-jen, Chung-yung yen-
chiu (Taipei: Wei-hsüeh Press, 1964), pp. 1-4. It
should be noted that Tsai's remarks are, in part,
based on Ts'ai Yün-chen's Chung-yung ch'an wei (Taipei: Chien-k'ang Book Co., 1956), preface, pp. 5-8.
Also see Ch'en P'an, Ta-hsüeh Chung-yung chin-shih
(Taipei: Cheng-chung Book Co., 1973), 2:97-111.

14. As Ts'ai Ai-jen points out in his Chung-
yung yen-chiu (p. 2), Ch'en Yüan-te simply assumes
that Tai Sheng is the author of Chung-yung. See
Ch'en Yüan-te, Chung-kuo ku-tai che-hsüeh shih
(Taipei: Chung-hua Book Co., 1962), pp. 398-400.

15. Yü Cheng-hsieh, "Chung-yung Ta-hsüeh"
in K'uei-ssu ts'un-kao (1884 edition), 2:21b-22.

16. For Ts'ui Shu's account, see his Chu-Ssu
k'ao-hsin yü-lu, in Ts'ui Tung-pi i-shu (1824 blockprint edition), 3:9a-12b, Ts'ui also criticized Chu
Hsi for grouping Chung-yung and Ta-hsüeh (Great
Learning) together with the Analects and Mencius.
In Ts'ui's view, Chu Hsi's elevation of the importance of the Four Books above that of the Five
Classics significantly distorted the original
structure of classical Confucianism. For a brief
reference to this, see Ts'ui Shu, K'ao-hsin lu t'i-
yao (reprint; Shanghai: Commercial Press, 1937)
1:19. For a general discussion on this controversy
in English, see Fung Yu-lan, A History of Chinese
Philosophy, 2 vols., trans. by Derk Bodde (Princeton: Princeton University Press, 1952), 1:369-371.

17. Chung-yung may have occasionally been
regarded as an independent treatise since the Han
dynasty--the "I-wen chih" in the Han-shu lists a
two-chapter Chung-yung shuo, and the "Ching-chi
chih" in the Sui-shu also lists a two-chapter
Chung-yung chuan by Tai Yung of Liu Sung (581-619),

a one-chapter Chung-yung chiang-shu by Liang Wu-ti,
and a five-chapter Ssu-chi chih-chih Chung-yung i
by an anonymous author. But before Chu Hsi's com-
pilation of the Four Books, Chung-yung had generally been treated as the thirty-first chapter of Li-
chi. However, Mao Ch'i-ling claimed that by the
time of the Liang dynasty in the fifth century the
two chapters of Li-chi, Ta-hsüeh and Chung-yung
had already been grouped together with the Analects
and Mencius. And the "four books" were then re-
ferred to as the "Small Classics" (hsiao-ching).
See Mao's "Chung-yung shuo," 5 chüan, in his Hsi-
ho ho-chi (1770 blockprint edition), vol. 38, 1:
1a-b.

        18. According to the standard historical
account, in 1027 on the occasion of the imperial
reception for the successful candidates of the
metropolitan examination, the emperor presented
a collection of his own poems and a copy of Chung-
yung as gifts. The copies of Chung-yung had been
prepared by the palace secretaries in advance.
Wang Yao-ch'en as the top scholar (chuang-yuan)
of the year might have received a copy of Chung-
yung in the calligraphic style of the emperor
himself. See Li T'ao, Hsü Tzu-chih t'ung-chien
ch'ang-pien (1881 blockprint edition), 161:9.

        19. Fan Chung-yen's instruction features
prominently in most of the biographical accounts
on Chang Tsai. In the minds of many historians,
Chang's early exposure to Chung-yung had a profound
impact on his intellectual development. See "Tao-
hsüeh chuan" in Sung-shih hsin-pien (1555 edition),
161:9.

        20. Ssu-ma Kuang's commentary is entitled
Chung-yung kuang-i. Actually, before Ssu-ma Kuang,
the T'ang philosopher Li Ao (fl. 798), and the
Northern Sung scholars, Hu Yuan (993-1059) and

Ch'iao Chih-chung, also wrote commentaries on
Chung-yung. Ssu-ma Kuang's contemporaries, the
Ch'eng brothers (Ch'eng Hao, 1032-1085, and Ch'eng
I, 1033-1077), were instrumental in elevating
Chung-yung to the status of a basic Confucian
classic. See Huang Te-ken, Chung-yung hsin-chieh
(Hong Kong: Shih-yung Book Co., 1967), Preface.

21. Actually, their argument is well summa-
rized by Fung Yu-lan as follows: "Toward the latter
part of Chung-yung, however, there occurs the sentence: 'Today throughout the empire carts all have
wheels with the same gauge; all writing is with the
same characters; and for conduct there exist the
same rules' (XXXVIII:3). This would seem to indicate conditions as they were following the unification of feudal China, first under Ch'in in 221
B.C., and later under the Han dynasty. The Chung-
yung also remarks elsewhere: 'It (the earth) sustains mountains like the Hua peak without feeling
their weight' (XXVI:9). This is a reference to the
sacred mountain of Hua-shan in Shensi, whereas it
would be natural to expect such a man as Tzu-ssu,
who was a native of the state of Lu (occupying what
is now Shantung), to refer in such a case to Shantung's sacred mountain, T'ai-shan. The statements
made on such philosophic concepts as Fate (ming),
man's nature (hsing), sincerity (ch'eng) and enlightenment (ming), are also more detailed than
those of Mencius, and would seem to be further developments of his doctrines, whereas Tzu-ssu lived
prior to Mencius. All this evidence would seem to
indicate that the Chung-yung was really the work
of a Confucian of Mencius' group, living in the
Ch'in or Han dynasty." See Fung Yu-lan, p. 370.
It should be noted that some minor stylistic
changes have been made in the above quotation.
Hu Shih, however, totally rejected this inter-

pretation. See his <u>Chung-kuo che-hsüeh-shih ta-kang</u> (Shanghai: Commercial Press, 1930), pp. 280-288.

22. See Ch'ien Mu, "Chung-yung hsin-i," <u>Min-chu p'ing-lun</u>, 6.16 (August 1955):2-8. As expected, Ch'ien's provocative article engendered much debate on the subject. For a perceptive critique of Ch'ien's interpretation, see Huang Chang-chien, "Tu Ch'ien Pin-ssu hsien-sheng 'Chung-yung hsin-i,'" <u>Min-chu p'ing-lun</u>, 7.1 (January 1956): 4-7, 21. For Ch'ien's response, see "'Chung-yung hsin-i' shen-shih" in the same issue, pp. 8-12.

23. See Ts'ai Ai-jen, Preface, p. 4. Actually, it is commonly accepted that <u>Chung-yung</u> "in the direction of a Confucian metaphysics served as a bridge between this [the Confucian] school, on the one hand, and Taoism and Buddhism on the other," Wm. T. de Bary, Wing-tsit Chan, and Burton Watson, comps., <u>Sources of Chinese Tradition</u>, 2 vols. (New York: Columbia University Press, 1960), 1:118. It should also be noted that <u>Chung-yung</u> has been taken seriously by modern Buddhist thinkers as well. See Ou-yang Chien's commentary on <u>Chung-yung</u> in <u>Ou-yang Chin-wu hsien-sheng nei-wai hsüeh</u> (Szechwan: Chih-na <u>nei-hsüeh-yuan</u>, 1941), vol. 14.

24. <u>Ta-hsüeh</u>, the shortest Confucian classic, contains only 1,747 words.

25. Other alternatives include Li Li-wu's division into fifteen chapters and Kuan Chih-tao's division into thirty-five chapters. See Ts'ai Ai-jen, pp. 4-6.

26. For a general discussion on the idea of <u>chün-tzu</u>, see W. Scott Morton, "The Confucian Concept of Man: The Original Formulation," <u>Philosophy East and West</u> 21 (January 1971):69-77.

27. Professor Lao Ssu-kuang of the Chinese University in Hong Kong prefers the translation of

ch'eng as "full realization."

28. See E. R. Hughes, trans., The Great
Learning and the Mean-in-Action, pp. 105-144.
Professor Hughes' reason for this translation is
worth noting: "This work is commonly known among
English-speaking people as The Doctrine of the
Mean. This is open to objection: the Chinese
title is Chung Yung; chung meaning 'centrality,'
yung meaning 'commonly and generally active.' To
translate chung as if the centrality conceived
were via the image of a bull's-eye in a target is
attractive but probably wrong. A mean of truth
between exaggerations of error represents more
what the author had in mind. To translate yung as
'functioning' also is attractive, but it is doubt-
ful whether the author had the biologist's notion
of functioning. I have, therefore, given the book's
English name as The Mean-in-action," p. 1, note 1.
It should also be noted that Hughes has made an
impressive attempt to outline the "purpose" behind
Chung-yung wherein the "mean-in-action" is also
understood as "the functioning centrality in life,"
p. 97. Also see Ku Hung-ming, trans., "Central
Harmony" (originally published as the Conduct of
Life; London: John Murray, 1906), in Lin Yutang,
ed. and trans., The Wisdom of Confucius (New York:
Modern Library, 1938), pp. 104-134. It should be
noted that the same translation by Ku is entitled
"The Golden Mean of Tsesze," in Lin Yutang, ed.,
The Wisdom of China and India (New York: Random
House, 1942), pp. 845-864. A reference to Ezra
Pound's rendition of Chung-yung as "Standing Fast
in the Middle" is found in Donald Davie, Ezra
Pound: Poet as Sculptor (New York: Oxford Uni-
versity Press, 1964), p. 182. Actually Pound is
known to have rendered Chung-yung as "the un-

wobbling pivot"; see Ezra Pound, trans. and commentary, Confucius: The Great Digest and Unwobbling Pivot (New York: New Directions, 1951), pp. 95-187. Pound's "note" to his rather idiosyncratic translation of Chung-yung is fascinating: "The second of the Four Classics, Chung Yung, The Unwobbling Pivot, contains what is usually supposed not to exist, namely the Confucian metaphysics. It is divided into three parts: the axis; the process; and sincerity, the perfect word, or the precise word; into Metaphysics: 'Only the most absolute sincerity under heaven can effect any change'; Politics: 'In cutting an axe-handle the model is not far off, in this sense: one holds one axe-handle while chopping the other. Thus one uses men in governing men'; Ethics: 'The archer, when he misses the bullseye, turns and seeks the cause of the error in himself.'" Unfortunately, these insightful observations are not developed in his commentary. And the translation itself is incomplete: "Twenty-four centuries ago Tsze Sze needed to continue his comment with a profession of faith, stating what the Confucian idea would effect; looking back now over the millennial history of China there is need neither of adjectives nor of comment. And for that reason I end my translation at this point, temporarily at least," p. 189.

29. For a perceptive discussion on this, see Hsü Fu-kuan, "Chung-yung te ti-wei wen-t'i," Min-chu p'ing lun 7.5 (March 1956):2-7, 22. The article is reprinted in Hsü's collected essays, Hsüeh-shu yü cheng-chih chih-chien (Taichung: Chung-yang Book Co., 1963), 2:118-134. For a succinct account of the same issue, see Shimada Kenji, Daigaku Chūyō (Tokyo: Asahi Shinbun, 1967), pp. 163-166. Also, see Iwakoshi Gen'ichirō, Chūyō shinkai (Tokyo: Mintoku Publishing Co., 1964), pp. 28-47.

30. Cheng's statement is quoted by K'ung

Ying-ta, in "Li-chi cheng-i," see K'ung Ying-ta, ed., Shih-san ching chu-shu (Kiangsi: Nan-ch'ang fu-hsüeh, 1815). 52:1.

31. Ch'eng I's statement is found in Chu Hsi's preface to Chung-yung chang-chü in Ssu-shu chi-chu. See Wing-tsit Chan, p. 97.

32. Ts'ai Ai-jen states that Kuo Chung-hsiao's remark is found in Chu I-ts'un's Ching-i k'ao, in which Chu quotes Kuo's remark from Li Li-wu. See Ts'ai Ai-jen, p. 9. Actually, since Kuo was a prominent disciple of Ch'eng I, his biography and thought are included in the Sung-Yüan hsüeh-an. For this particular remark, see "Chien-shan hsüeh-an," in the Sung-Yuan hsüeh-an, 4 vols. (reprint; Shanghai: Commercial Press, 1934), 2:28:98.

33. See his preface to the Chung-yung chang-chü. For a systematic discussion of Chu Hsi's approach and method in the study of the Four Books, see Ch'ien Mu, Chu Tzu hsin hsüeh-an, 4:180-229.

34. I am aware that "commonality," like the word "mean," is not an ideal translation of the Confucian concept of "yung." However, in ordinary language, yung is often associated with notions such as "common," "usual," "ordinary," "simple," and "unchanging." And it is not infrequently used in a derogatory sense. In the course of our discussion, it should become clear that the technical usage of "yung" as a great Confucian virtue specifically refers to commonly shared experiences. It is the Confucian belief that the ultimate meaning of life is rooted in the ordinary human existence. Thus, "commonality," which means commonness, frequency, and common people without authority and rank, is a close approximation of yung.

35. For a scholarly reflection on this matter, see Hsü Fu-kuan, "Chung-yung te tsai k'ao-ch'a," Min-chu p'ing-lun, 13 (August 1962):9-14. For

an extremely provocative study of Chung-yung in
the light of Hsün Tzu's philosophy of mind, see
Li Hsiang-yin, "Chung-yung t'u-chieh" in Ju-hsüeh
tsai shih-chieh lun-wen chi (Hong Kong: Tung-fang
jen-wen hsüeh-hui, 1969), pp. 23-87.

36. See Hsü Fu-kuan, Hsüeh-shu yü cheng-chih
chih-chien, 2:120-121.

37. For reference to Huang's article, see
note 20.

38. See Ch'en P'an, "Chung-yung pien-i," Min-
chu p'ing-lun, 5 (December 1954):3-7, 13. Ch'en's
analysis can also be regarded as a definitive answer
to the question of authorship raised by Fung Yu-lan,
and, for that matter, by the Ch'ing scholars. For
Fung's summary of the interpretation advanced by
the Ch'ing scholars, see note 19.

39. When Tseng Tzu was gravely ill, he called
to him his disciples and said, "Uncover my feet,
uncover my hands. It is said in the Book of Poetry,
'We should be apprehensive and cautious, as if on
the brink of a deep gulf, as if treading on thin
ice,' and so have I been. Now and hereafter, I
know my escape from all injury to my person, O ye,
my little children." See Analects, VIII:3. The
translation of Tseng Tzu's statement is based on
James Legge, trans., The Chinese Classics, Vol.
I: Confucian Analects (reprint; Taipei: Wen-
hsing Book Co., 1966), p. 208. It should be noted
that Tseng Tzu's instruction to his disciples about
the difficult task of constantly observing the
virtue of filial piety by cautiously taking care
of one's body is very much in accord with Chung-
yung's idea of being "watchful over oneself when
one is alone."

40. This is based on the following statement
in the Analects (XIV:25): "In ancient times, men
learned with a view to their own improvement.

Now-a-days, men learn with a view to the appro-
bation of others," in James Legge, trans., <u>The
Chinese Classics</u>, 1:285. Actually the expression
"<u>wei-chi</u>" can be rendered as "for his (their) own
sake" and that of "<u>wei-jen</u>" "for the sake of
others."

Notes to Chapter 2

1. It should be noted that the Chinese word chung, which is commonly pronounced in the first tone as an adjective to mean "central" or "middle," can also be pronounced in the fourth tone as a verb to mean "hit the center" or "attain the goal." In this particular connection, the principle of centrality signifies the way of being able to act in accordance with the best possible structure of affairs in a given situation. In the course of our discussion, it should become clear that this is closely associated with the idea that a self-rectified archer is capable of hitting the bull's eye because of his inner strength and perfect timing. For a brief explanation of this point, see Tu Wei-ming, "An Introductory Note on Time and Temporality," Philosophy East and West 24 (April 1974):119, 122. It should also be mentioned that occasionally chung is better translated as "centeredness."

2. Indeed, as the Book of Odes says, "In hewing an axe-handle, in hewing an axe-handle, the pattern is not far off." Commenting on this verse, Chung-yung states, "If we take an axe handle to hew another axe handle and look askance from one to the other, we may still think the pattern is far away," but "the Way is not far away from man. When a man pursues the Way and yet remains away from man, his course cannot be considered the Way" [XIII:2]. Cf. Donald Munro, The Concept of Man in Early China (Stanford, Ca.: Stanford University Press, 1969), pp. 96-99.

3. See K'ung Ying-ta, "Li-chi chu-shu," 52: 10a-b, in Shih-san ching chu-shu (reprint; Taipei: I-wen Press, 1815 edition), 8:883.

4. For a perceptive discussion on this concept, see Hsü Fu-kuan, "Yu-kuan Chung-kuo ssu-hsiang-shih chung i-ko chi-t'i te k'ao-ch'ao--shih Lun-yü 'wu-shih erh chih t'ien-ming,'" in his Hsüeh-shu yü cheng-chih chih-chien (Taichung: Chung-yang Book Co., 1963), 2:153-166. The article originally appeared in Min-chu p'ing-lun 7.16 (August 1956):2-6, 12.

5. Analects, XIV:41.

6. Analects, IV:15. See Wing-tsit Chan's comment on this point in his A Source Book (Princeton, N.J.: Princeton University Press, 1973), p. 27.

7. Analects, XII:2.

8. Analects, VI:10. The statement reads: "Jan Ch'iu said, It is not that your Way does not commend itself to me, but that it demands powers I do not possess. The Master said, He whose strength gives out collapses during the course of the journey [the Way]; but you deliberately draw the line." See Arthur Waley, trans., The Analects of Confucius (London: George Allen & Unwin, Ltd., 1938), p. 118. See also the distinction between unwillingness and inability in Mencius, IA:7.

9. Analects, XIV:4. For a brief discussion of this, see Tu Wei-ming, "On the Spiritual Development of Confucius' Personality," Thought and Word 11 (September 1973):35-36.

10. For a perceptive analysis of this issue, see T'ang Chün-i, "The Development of Ideas of Spiritual Value in Chinese Philosophy," in Charles A. Moore, ed., The Chinese Mind (Honolulu: East-West Center Press, 1967), pp. 192-193.

11. Analects, IX:10.

12. Analects, VI:28.

13. Analects, XII:2.

1. For a general discussion on this point,
see Tu Wei-ming, "Li as Process of Humanization,"
Philosophy East and West 22 (April 1972):188-190.

2. Confucius' disciple, Tseng Tzu, is alleged
to have said, "When proper respect towards the dead
is shown at the End and continued after they are
far away the virtue of the people will become en-
riched," Analects, I:9. For a detailed discussion
of the Confucian mourning rituals, see the "Tseng
Tzu wen" chapter in Li-chi, annotated by Wang
Meng-o (Taipei: Commercial Press, 1971), 7:243-
271.

3. The following statement, attributed to
Confucius' disciple Yu Tzu, has often been cited to
support this claim: "Few of those who are filial
sons and respectful brothers will show disrespect
to superiors, and there has never been a man who is
not disrespectful to superiors and yet creates
disorder. A superior man is devoted to the funda-
mentals [the root]. When the root is firmly established, the moral law [Tao] will grow. Filial
piety and brotherly respect are the root of humanity
(jen)," Analects, I:2. See Wing-tsit Chan, A Source
Book in Chinese Philosophy (Princeton, N.J.:
Princeton University Press, 1973), pp. 19-20. However, it seems obvious that in Yu Tzu's statement,
filial piety, like brotherly love, is considered a
basic form of respect upon which humanity can be
fully realized. The relationship between filial
piety as an ethicoreligious sentiment and obedience
as a manifestation of political loyalty is, at
best, tenuous.

4. The following statement is a case in point:
"The Duke of She told Confucius, 'In my country

there is an upright man named Kung. When his father stole a sheep, he bore witness against him.' Confucius said, 'The upright men in my community are different from this. The father conceals the misconduct of the son and the son conceals the misconduct of the father. Uprightness is to be found in this,'" Analects, XIII:18. See Wing-tsit Chan, p. 41. Although the example has frequently been used to show that Confucius preferred nepotism (a form of particularism) to universalism, the intention here seems simply to signify that to sacrifice the father-son relationship for a relatively minor offense is not in keeping with the spirit of uprightness.

5. Mencius said, "There are three things which are unfilial, and to have no posterity (hou) is the greatest of them all. Shun married without first informing his parents lest he have no posterity. Superior men consider this as if he had informed his parents," Mencius, IVA:26. According to Chao Ch'i's commentary, the other two unfilial acts are to obey parents blindly and thus cause them to become unrighteous, and to refuse to serve in the government for emolument when one's parents are old and one's family poor. See Wing-tsit Chan, pp. 75-76. To understand this remark in the context of Shun's marriage, see Mencius, VA:2.

6. Analects, VII:1.

7. Analects, VII:1.

8. See Confucius' reference to King Wen in Analects, VIII:20.

9. For a brief account of King Wen's alleged contribution to the formation of the Book of Changes, see The I Ching, translated into German by Richard Wilhelm and rendered into English by Cary F. Baynes (Princeton, N.J: Princeton University Press, 1972), Introduction, pp. liii and lix.

10. For a vivid account of King Wu's alleged expedition against the Shang tyrant, see "Chou pen-chi," in Ssu-ma Ch'ien's Shih-chi (reprint; Peking: Chung-hua Book Co., 1959), IV:120-126.

11. Actually, as stated in the Shih-chi (IV: 120-123), King Wu's campaign against the last king of the Shang dynasty was launched more than a year after the death of his father. However, according to the Confucian ritual, a proper burial for one's parent should involve a three-year mourning period; see Analects, XVII:21.

12. See Ssu-ma Ch'ien, Shih-chi, IV:132. Also see the "Chin-t'eng" chapter in Shang-shu, annotated by Ch'u Wan-li (Taipei: Commercial Press, 1971), p. 87.

13. See the "Yao-tien" chapter in Shang-shu, p. 8. For a brief account of the legend of Shun as understood by Mencius, see D. C. Lau, trans., Mencius (London: Penguin Classics, 1970), pp. 223-227.

14. See Mencius, VA:2. For an English translation, see D. C. Lau, pp. 139-140.

15. The expression is taken from the following statement in Mencius:

What is the most important duty? One's duty towards one's parents. What is the most important thing to watch over? One's own character. I have heard of a man who, not having allowed his character to be morally lost, is able to discharge his duties towards his parent; but I have not heard of one morally lost who is able to do so. There are many duties one should discharge, but the fulfillment of one's duty towards one's parents is the most basic. There are many things one should watch over, but watching over one's character is the most basic.

Tseng Tzu, in looking after Tseng Hsi [this
is the father of Tseng Tzu, not to be confused
with the Tseng Hsi who was Tseng Tzu's younger
son], saw to it that he always had meat and
drink, and, on clearing away the food, always
asked to whom it should be given. When asked
whether there was any food left, he always re-
plied in the affirmative. After Tseng Hsi's
death, when Tseng Yüan looked after Tseng Tzu,
he, too, saw to it that he always had meat and
drink, but, on clearing away the food, never
asked to whom it should be given. When asked
whether there was any food left, he always re-
plied in the negative. He did this so that
the left-over food could be served up again.
This can only be described as looking after the
mouth and belly (yang k'ou-t'i). Someone like
Tseng Tzu can truly be said to be solicitous
of the wishes of his parent (yang-chih). One
does well if one can emulate the way Tseng Tzu
treated his parent.

Mencius, IVA:19. See D. C. Lau, pp. 125-126.

16. Mencius, IVA:19. Cf. the Confucian saying that if for the whole three years of mourning
a son manages to carry on the way of his father, he
is a filial son indeed, Analects, IV:20.

17. Mencius, IVB:13. See D. C. Lau, p. 130.

18. Analects, II:7. See Wm. T. de Bary,
Wing-tsit Chan, and Burton Watson, comps., Sources
of Chinese Tradition (New York: Columbia University
Press, 1960), 1:27.

19. Analects, I:9. See James Legge, trans.,
The Chinese Classics, Vol. I: Confucian Analects
(reprint; Taipei: Wen-hsing Book Co., 1966), p. 141.

20. Analects, III:17.

21. Analects, IV:13.

22. _Analects_, XII:17. Also see Confucius' discussion on the priority of the rectification of names in the establishment of a good government, _Analects_, XIII:3 and XII:2.

23. _Analects_, XII:19.

24. See Wing-tsit Chan, p. 104.

25. _Mencius_, VIIB:16. See Wing-tsit Chan, p. 81.

26. For a succinct analysis of Mencius' theory of human nature, see T'ang Chün-i, _Chung-kuo che-hsüeh yüan-lun: yüan-hsing p'ien_ (Hong Kong: New Asia Research Institute, 1968), pp. 20-32. Also see Donald Munro, _The Concept of Man in Early China_ (Stanford, Ca.: Stanford University Press, 1969), pp. 74-77.

27. This is part of the reason why Mencius severely criticizes Mo Tzu's concept of "universal love." See _Mencius_, IIIB:9. Also see D. C. Lau, _Mencius_, p. 114.

28. Part of the Mencian statement reads: "Humanity is man's peaceful abode and righteousness his proper path. It is indeed lamentable for anyone not to live in his peaceful abode and not to follow his proper path." See _Mencius_, IVA:10. Cf. D. C. Lau, p. 122.

29. Tu Wei-ming, "_Li_ as Process of Humanization," _Philosophy East and West_ 22 (April 1972):194.

30. The "eight steps" of the _Great Learning_ are: (1) investigation of things, (2) extension of knowledge, (3) sincerity of the will, (4) rectification of the mind, (5) cultivation of personal life, (6) regulation of family, (7) bringing order to the state, and (8) bringing peace throughout the world. See Wing-tsit Chan, pp. 86-87.

31. It should also be noted that it is precisely in this connection that Mencius argued that

tyrannicide is not regicide: "King Hsüan of Ch'i
asked, 'Is it true that T'ang banished Chieh and
King Wu marched against Tchou?' 'It is so recorded,'
answered Mencius. 'Is regicide permissible?' 'A
man who mutilates benevolence is a mutilator, while
one who cripples rightness is a crippler. He who is
both a mutilator and a crippler is an "outcast." I
have indeed heard of the punishment of the "outcast
Tchou," but I have not heard of any regicide,'" Mencius, IB:8. See D. C. Lau, p. 68.

32. Mencius, III:4. See Wing-tsit Chan, pp.
69-70. Italics added.

33. Wing-tsit Chan, A Source Book, p. 30.

34. Analects, IV:2. Note that Wing-tsit Chan
renders the same passage as "The man of humanity is
naturally at ease with humanity. The man of wisdom
cultivates humanity for its advantage," A Source Book,
p. 25.

35. Analects, VI:28. See Wing-tsit Chan, p.
31.

36. Analects, VI:28. See Wing-tsit Chan, p.
31.

37. Analects, V:11, VI:28, and XII:2.

38. For a succinct, if not completely accurate,
account of the distinction between wang (king) and
pa (hegemon), see Arthur Waley, trans., The Analects
of Confucius (London: George Allen & Unwin, Ltd.,
1938), pp. 47-50. Also see Mencius, VIB:7.

39. Analects, XII:1.

40. Analects, I:12. See Wing-tsit Chan, p. 21.

41. For a brief discussion on this issue, see
Shimada Kenji, Chūyō Daigaku (Tokyo: Asahi Shinbun,
1967), p. 275.

42. The following statement is a case in
point: "It was because Chieh and Chou lost the
people that they lost the empire, and it was because

they lost the hearts of the people that they lost
the people. Here is the way to win the empire: win
the people and you win the empire. Here is the way
to win the people: win their hearts and you win the
people. Here is the way to win their hearts: give
them and share with them what they like, and do not
do to them what they do not like. The people turn to
a humane ruler as water flows downward or beasts take
to wilderness," Mencius, IVA:9. See Wm. T. de Bary,
Wing-tsit Chan, and Burton Watson, p. 93. Also see
the well-known statement "Heaven sees with the eyes
of its people. Heaven hears with the ears of its
people," quoted from Shang-shu by Mencius to explicate the "Mandate of Heaven" idea, Mencius, VA:5.
Cf. D. C. Lau, pp. 143-144.

43. See Shimada Kenji, p. 277. His reference
to a similar statement in Chou-li is particularly
suggestive. See Chou-li, annotated by Lin Yin
(Taipei: Commercial Press, 1972), pp. 333-334.

44. Analects, XII:5.

45. For example, see Mencius, IA:3.

46. The following statement is a case in
point: "Yü looked upon himself as responsible for
anyone in the empire who drowned; Chi looked upon
himself as responsible for anyone in the empire who
starved. That is why they went about their tasks
with such a sense of urgency," Mencius, IVB:29. See
D. C. Lau, pp. 134-135.

Notes to Chapter 4

1. For Nietzsche's position on this issue, see his Human, All-Too-Human, in The Complete Works of Friedrich Nietzsche, ed. Oscar Levy, (New York: Russell & Russell, Inc., 1964), vol. 6, part I, pp. 93-95.

2. See Nietzsche, pp. 93-95.

3. Immanuel Kant, Critique of Practical Reason, trans. Thomas K. Abbott (London: Longmans, Green & Co., 1909), p. 227.

4. Attributed to J. G. Fichte.

5. Reinhold Niebuhr, An Interpretation of Christian Ethics (New York: Harper & Brothers Publishers, 1935), p. 50.

6. J. J. Rousseau, Reply to Archbishop de Beaumont's Condemnation of the book Émile. See "Lettre de Jean-Jacques Rousseau, citoyen de Genéve, à Christophe de Beaumont, archeveque de Paris," in Rousseau, J. J., Oeuvres Complètes, ed. Bernard Gagnebin and Marcel Raymond; Bibliothèque de la Pléiade (Paris: Gallimard, 1964), IV:927-1007.

7. For an inspiring discussion on the creative nature of man from a Christian point of view, see S. L. Frank, Reality and Man: An Essay in the Meta-physics of Human Nature, trans. from the Russian by Natalie Duddington (New York: Taplinger Publishing Co., 1965), pp. 153-161. Also see Hsiung Shih-li's comment on the metaphysics of human nature in Chung-yung in his Tu-ching shih-yao, (reprint; Taipei: Kuang-wen Book Co., 1960), II:22. A comparable po-sition from K'ang Yu-wei's philosophy of the "great unity" (ta-t'ung) is found in his Chung-yung chu (reprint; Taipei: The Commercial Press, 1968), 26b-46b. For a balanced account on the same subject, see Ch'en Chu, Chung-yung chu-ts'an (Shanghai: Com-

mercial Press, 1930), pp. 46-74. It should be noted that in Ch'en Chu's study, in addition to the standard commentaries on <u>Chung-yung</u> by Ch'eng Hsüan, K'ung Yin-ta, and Chu Hsi, works on <u>Chung-yung</u> by Ku Yen-wu, Tai Chen, K'ang Yu-wei, Hsü Hao, Hsü Shao-chen, Liu Shih-p'ei, Ma Ch'i-ch'ang, T'ang Wei-chih, and Ch'en Chung-fan have also been consulted.

8. Wing-tsit Chan, <u>A Source Book of Chinese Philosophy</u>, (Princeton, N.J.: Princeton University Press, 1973), p. 96.

9. Wing-tsit Chan, p. 95. Of course, here Chan simply notes a commonly accepted point of view.

10. <u>Mencius</u>, IVA:12. See D. C. Lau, trans., <u>Mencius</u> (London: Penguin Classics, 1970), p. 123.

11. <u>Mencius</u>, VIIA:1. See D. C. Lau, p. 182.

12. <u>Mencius</u>, VIIA:4. See D. C. Lau, p. 182, but note that <u>jen</u> is here rendered as "humanity" rather than "benevolence." Italics added.

13. <u>Mencius</u>, VIIA:3. See D. C. Lau, p. 182.

14. Wing-tsit Chan, p. 96.

15. Wing-tsit Chan, p. 96.

16. "Duke Ai asked which of the disciples had a love of learning. Master K'ung answered him saying, There was Yen Hui. He had a great love of learning. He never vented his wrath upon the innocent nor let himself make the same mistake twice. Unfortunately the span of life allotted to him by Heaven was short, and he died. At present there are none or at any rate I have heard of none who are fond of learning," <u>Analects</u>, VI:2. See Arthur Waley, trans., <u>The Analects of Confucius</u> (London: George Allen & Unwin, Ltd., 1938), p. 115, but note <u>pu erh-kuo</u> is here rendered differently from "let others suffer for his faults." Also see <u>Analects</u>, XI:6.

17. <u>Mencius</u>, VIIA:16. See D. C. Lau, pp. 184-185.

18. <u>Analects</u>, VI:28.

19. Analects, XII:19.

20. This line can also be rendered as "these are attainments (virtues) of which our nature is capable."

21. However, the idea of ch'eng in Chung-yung comes very close to S. L. Frank's notion of God. See the chapter on "Man and God" in his Reality and Man, pp. 110-161.

22. Mencius, VIA:7.3 Note that the two sentences are rendered by D. C. Lau as follows: "The sage and I are of the same kind" and "The sage is simply the man first to discover this common element in my heart," p. 164. It should be pointed out that the Chinese character used here is t'ung (same or common).

23. Analects, VI:28.

24. Analects, II:23 and III:14.

25. For a general discussion on the religious import of the Confucian concept of li (ritual), see Herbert Fingarette, "Human Community as Holy Rite: An Interpretation of Confucius' Analects," Harvard Theological Review (January 1966):53-68. A perceptive analysis of the same concept in the context of classical Confucian thought is found in Fingarette's superb study on Confucius--The Secular as Sacred (New York: Harper & Row, 1972), pp. 1-82. Also see Huston Smith, "Transcendence in Traditional China," Religious Studies, 2 (1966-67):185-196.

26. Mencius, VB:1. See D. C. Lau, p. 150.

27. Mencius, VIIB:25. See D. C. Lau, p. 199.

28. Analects, XIV:25.

Glossary

Ai 哀

Akatsuka Kiyoshi 赤塚忠

Asahi Shinbun 朝日新聞

Chang Tsai 張載

Chao Ch'i 趙岐

Chao Yüeh-chih 晁説之

Ch'en Chu 陳柱

Ch'en Chung-fan 陳鐘凡

Ch'en P'an 陳槃

Ch'en Yüan-te 陳元德

cheng (rectification) 正

cheng (politics) 政

cheng (evident) 徵

Cheng-chung 正中

Cheng Hsüan 鄭玄

ch'eng 誠

Ch'eng Hao 程顥

Ch'eng I 程頤

ch'eng-wu 成物

Chi (Minister of Agriculture under Shun) 稷

Chi (King Wen's father) 季

chi 繼

Ch'i 齊

Ch'i-sung 契嵩

Ch'iao Chih-chung 喬執中

Chieh 桀

Chien-k'ang 建康

"Chien-shan hsüeh-an" 蕺山學案

Ch'ien Mu 錢穆

chih 志

Chih-na nei-hsüeh yüan 支那內學院

Chih-yüan 智圓

Chin-ssu lu 近思錄

"Chin-t'eng" 金縢

Ch'in 秦

ch'in 親

ching 經

"Ching-chi chih" 經籍志

"Ching-i k'ao" 經義考

Ch'ing 清

chiu 久

Chou (dynasty) 周

Chou (last king of Shang) 紂

Chou-li 周禮

"Chou pen-chi" 周本紀

Chu Hsi 朱熹

Chu I-ts'un 朱彝尊

Chu Tzu hsin hsüeh-an 朱子新學案

Ch'ü Wan-li 屈萬里

Chuang Tzu 莊子

chuang-yüan 狀元

chün-tzu 君子

chung (centrality) 中

chung (loyalty) 忠

Chung-hua 中華

Chung-kuo che-hsüeh 中國哲學
    ta-kang 大綱

Chung-kuo che-hsüeh yüan-lun: 中國哲學原論
    yüan-hsing p'ien 原性篇

Chung-kuo ku-tai che-hsüeh shih 中國古代哲學史

Chung-ni 仲尼

Chung-yang 中央

Chung-yung ch'an-wei 中庸闡微

Chung-yung chang-chü 中庸章句

Chung-yung chiang shu 中庸講疏

Chung-yung chu 中庸注

Chung-yung chu-ts'an 中庸注參

Chung-yung chuan 中庸傳

Chung-yung hsin-i 中庸新義

Chung-yung hsin-i shen-shih 中庸新義申釋

Chung-yung kuang-i 中庸廣義

Chung-yung pien-i 中庸辯疑

Chung-yung shuo 中庸説

Chung-yung Ta-hsüeh 中庸大學

"Chung-yung te ti-wei wen-t'i" 中庸的地位問題

"Chung-yung te tsai k'ao-ch'a" 中庸的再考察

"Chung-yung t'u-chieh" 中庸圖解

Chung-yung yen-chiu 中庸研究

Chūyō shinkai 中庸新解

Daigaku Chūyō 大學中庸

Fan Chung-yen 范仲淹

fu-wu 覆物

Fung Yu-lan 馮友蘭

Han 漢

Han-shu 漢書

hao-hsüeh 好學

hou 後

Hsia 夏

hsiao 孝

Hsieh 契

hsien 賢

hsien-neng 賢能

Hsin-t'i yü hsing-t'i 心體與性體

hsing 性

Hsiung Shih-li 熊十力

hsü 序

Hsü Fu-kuan 徐復觀

Hsü Hao 徐灝

Hsü Shao-chen 徐紹楨

Hsü Tzu-chih t'ung-chien 續資治通鑑
　　ch'ang-pien 長編

Hsüan 宣

Hsüeh-shu yü cheng-chih 學術與政治
　　chih-chien 之間

Hsün Tzu 荀子

Hu Shih 胡適

Hu Yüan 胡瑗

Hua 華

Hua-shan 華山

Huang Chang-chien 黃彰健

Huang Te-kuan 黃德根

i 義

I Ching 易經

I-wen 藝文

"I-wen chih" 藝文志

Iwakoshi Gen'ichirō 岩越元一郎

Jan Ch'iu 冉求

jen (person) 人

jen (humanity) 仁

jen-lu 人路

Jen-tsung 仁宗

Ju-chia te chung-ho kuan 儒家的中和觀

Ju-hsüeh tsai shih-chieh 儒家在世界

　　lun-wen chi 論文集

ju-te 入德

K'ang Yu-wei 康有為

kao-ming 高明

Ku Hung-ming 辜鴻銘

Ku Yen-wu 顧炎武

Kuan Chih-tao 管志道

Kuang-wen 廣文

K'uei-ssu ts'un-kao 癸巳存稿

Kung 躬

kung-fu 工夫

K'ung Chi 孔伋

K'ung Ying-ta 孔穎達

Kuo Chung-hsiao 郭忠孝

li 禮

Li Ao 李翱

Li-chi 禮記

Li-chi cheng-i 禮記正義

Li-chi chu-shu 禮記注疏

Li Hsiang-yin 李相殷

Li Kuang-ti 李光地

Li Li-wu 黎立武

Li T'ao 李燾

Liang 梁

Liang Wu-ti 梁武帝

Lin Yin 林尹

Liu Shih-p'ei 劉師培

Liu Shu-hsien 劉述先

Liu Sung 劉宋

Lu 魯

Lü Tsu-ch'ien 呂祖謙

Lung-meng 龍門

Ma Ch'i-ch'ang 馬其昶

Meiji sho-in 明治書院

Meitoku 明德、

Mou Tsung-san 牟宗三

Min-chu p'ing-lun 民主評論

Ming 明

ming (enlightenment, brilliance) 明

ming (mandate, fate) 命

Mo Tzu 墨子

Nan-ch'ang fu-hsüeh 南昌府學

Ou-yang Chin-wu hsien-sheng 歐陽竟无先生

     nei-wai hsüeh 内外學

Ou-yang Chien 歐陽漸

pa 霸

Pan Ku 班固

p'ei-t'ien 配天

pen-t'i 本體

pieh 別

po-hou 博厚

po-shih 博士

pu erh-kuo 不貳過

pu-hsi 不息

San-min 三民

Shang 商

Shang-shu 尚書

She 葉

shen-tu 慎獨

sheng-sheng pu-hsi 生生不息

shih 事

Shih-chi 史記

Shih-san ching chu-shu 十三經注疏

Shih-yung 實用

Shimada Kenji 島田虔次

Shinyaku kambun taikei 新釋漢文大系

shu (altruism) 恕

shu (transmit) 述

Shūei sha 集英社

Shun 舜

shun 純

Ssu-chi chih-chih Chung-yung i 私記制旨中庸義

Ssu-ma Ch'ien 司馬遷

Ssu-ma Kuang 司馬光

ssu-pu pei-yao 四部備要

Ssu-shu chi-chu 四書集注

ssu-tuan 四端

Sui 隋

Sui-shu 隋書

Sung 宋

Sung-shih hsin-pien 宋史新編

Sung-Yüan hsüeh-an 宋元學案

ta-hsiao (great filiality) 大孝

ta-hsiao (extending filiality) 達孝

Ta-hsüeh Chung-yung chin shih 大學中庸今釋

ta-tao 達道

ta-te 達德

ta-t'ung 大同

Tai Chen 戴震

Tai Sheng 戴聖

Tai Yung 戴顒

T'ai 太

T'ai-shan 泰山

T'ang 湯

T'ang Chün-i 唐君毅

T'ang Wei-chih 唐蔚芝

"Tao-hsüeh chuan" 道學傳

tao-te ti hsing-erh-shang hsüeh 道德的形而上學

Tchou (same as Chou above) 紂

t'ien-te 天德

tsai-wu 載物

Ts'ai Ai-jen 蔡愛仁

Ts'ai Yün-chen 蔡運辰

Tseng Tzu 曾子

"Tseng Tzu wen" 曾子問

"Tu Ch'ien Pin-ssu hsien-sheng 讀錢賓四先生
　　　Chung-yung hsin-i" 中庸新義

Tu-ching shih-yao 讀經示要

tu-shu fa 讀書法

Tu Wei-ming 杜維明

Tung Chung-shu 董仲舒

Tung-fang jen-wen hsüeh-hui 東方人文學會

t'ung 同

Tzu Kung 子貢

Tzu Ssu 子思

Tz'u 賜

wang 王

Wang Meng-o 王夢鷗

Wang Yao-ch'en 王堯臣

Wang Yü 王煜

wei-chi 為己

wei-chi chih hsüeh 為己之學

wei-jen 為人

Wei-hsüeh 為學

Wen 文

Wen-hsing 文星

Wu 武

wu (awakening) 悟

wu (thing) 物

wu-ch'ang 五常

wu-lun 五倫

wu-mu pu-i 於穆不已

wu-te 五德

Wu-ti 武帝

Yamashita Ryūji 山下龍二

yang-chih 養志

yang k'ou-t'i 養口體

Yao 堯

"Yao-tien" 堯典

Yeh Yu 葉酉

Yen Hui 顏回

yu-chiu 悠久

"Yu-kuan Chung-kuo 有關中國
　　ssu-hsiang-shih chung 思想史中
　　i-ko chi-t'i te 一個基題的
　　k'ao-ch'a—shih Lun-yü 考察—釋論語
　　wu-shih erh chih-t'ien-ming" 五十而知天命

Yu Tzu 有子
Yü 禹
Yü Cheng-hsieh 俞正燮
Yü Yüeh 俞樾
Yuan Mei 袁枚
yung 庸
Yung Sung-bum 尹聖範
Zenyaku kambun taikei 全釋漢文大系

Tu Wei-ming is Associate Professor of History, University of California at Berkeley, where he offers courses on Chinese intellectual history and on the philosophies of China. Professor Tu was educated at Tunghai University and Harvard University (Ph.D., 1968), and has taught at Princeton University. His work on Neo-Confucian Thought in Action: Wang Yang-ming's Youth (1472-1509) is being prepared for publication by the University of California Press, and currently he is working on Chu Hsi.

�